Adolf Eichmann

Holocaust Heroes
and Nazi Criminals

Adolf Eichmann

Executing the "Final Solution"

Tom Streissguth

Enslow Publishers, Inc.
40 Industrial Road   PO Box 38
Box 398   Aldershot
Berkeley Heights, NJ 07922 Hants GU12 6BP
USA   UK
http://www.enslow.com

Library of Congress Cataloging-in-Publication Data:

Streissguth, Thomas, 1958–
    Adolf Eichmann : executing the "Final Solution" / Tom Streissguth.—1st ed.
      p. cm. — (Holocaust heroes and Nazi criminals)
    Includes bibliographical references and index.
    ISBN 0-7660-2575-6
      1. Eichmann, Adolf, 1906–1962—Juvenile literature. 2. Nazis—Biography—Juvenile
literature. 3. War criminals—Germany—Biography—Juvenile literature. 4. Holocaust,
Jewish (1939–1945)—Juvenile literature. 5. World War, 1939–1945—Atrocities—
Juvenile literature. I. Title. II. Series.
    DD247.E5S85 2005
    364.15′1′092—dc22

                                 2004028116

Printed in the United States of America

10 9 8 7 6 5 4 3 2 1

To Our Readers: We have done our best to make sure all Internet addresses in this book
were active and appropriate when we went to press. However, the author and the publisher
have no control over and assume no liability for the material available on those Internet
sites or on other Web sites they may link to. Any comments or suggestions can be sent by
e-mail to comments@enslow.com or to the address on the back cover.

Illustration Credits: Courtesy of the Simon Wiesenthal Center Library and Archives, Los
Angeles, Calif., p. 108; Courtesy of the USHMM Photo Archives, pp. 5, 7, 8, 9, 80, 84 (left),
90, 117, 142 (top and second from bottom), 143 (top), 145 (bottom), 147 (second from
bottom), 148, 152, 154, 157, 158; Enslow Publishers, Inc., p. 110; Hagstromer & Qviberg
Fondkommission, pp. 84 (right), 92; Harry Lore, courtesy of the USHMM Photo Archives,
p. 147 (top); The Israel Government Press Office, courtesy of the USHMM Photo Archives,
pp. 123, 130, 134, 138; James Blevins, courtesy of the USHMM Photo Archives, p. 33; James
Sanders, courtesy of the USHMM Photo Archives, p. 145 (top); KZ Gedenkstatte Dachau,
courtesy of USHMM, p. 127; Lorenz Schmuhl, courtesy of USHMM Photo Archives, pp. 142
(third from bottom), 146 (top), 147 (third from bottom); The Main Commission for the
Prosecution of Crimes Against the Polish Nation, courtesy of the USHMM Photo Archives,
pp. 142 (second from top), 146 (bottom), 147 (second from top); National Archives and
Records Administration, pp. 11, 21, 24, 44, 59, 65, 79, 101, 112, 142 (third from top), 144, 147
(third from top); The National Museum of American Jewish History, pp. 142 (bottom), 143
(bottom), 147 (bottom); Reproduced from the Collections of the Library of Congress, pp. 15,
16, 36, 41, 47, 52, 74, 96, 98.

Cover Illustration: Courtesy of the USHMM Photo Archives.

Contents

Acknowledgments

The author sincerely thanks the National Archives, the Library of Congress, the United States Holocaust Memorial Museum, and the Yad Vashem museum of Jerusalem for their assistance in the preparation of this book.

Fast Facts About Adolf Eichmann

Date of Birth: March 19, 1906

Place of Birth: Solingen, Germany

Civilian occupation: salesman, Vacuum Oil Company

Nazi party membership: 1932

Rank achieved: Obersturmbannführer

Department: Section IV B 4, RSHA

Family: Wife, Veronika Liebl (married 1935); sons Klaus, Horst, Dieter, Ricardo

Capture: May 11, 1960, Buenos Aires

Trial: April 11–December 15, 1961; sentenced to death by hanging

Death: May 31, 1962

Adolf Eichmann

Introduction: Eichmann on the Run

It was the early afternoon of Sunday, April 29, 1945. Brigadier General Henning Linden of the 42nd Infantry Division, U.S. Seventh Army, walked to the gates of a large compound. Tall wooden guard towers overlooked the camp, which was surrounded by barbed-wire fences. Nearby lay the village of Dachau in southern Germany.

Linden approached with caution. A battle between German guards and American troops had taken place in the morning. Men on both sides had been killed before the camp's defenders raised a white flag. Linden's troops still had their guns raised and ready when Second Lieutenant Heinrich Wicker, a German officer, approached the gates. With an aide at his side, Wicker formally surrendered the camp.

In the words of the official Seventh Army report:

> . . . the air was unusually still. The big field outside the compound was deserted. Suddenly someone began running toward the gate at the other side of the field. Others followed. The word was shouted through the mass of gray, tired prisoners. Americans! That word repeated, yelled over the shoulders in throaty Polish, in Italian, in Russian, and Dutch and in the familiar ring of French.[1]

The Dachau prisoners told their stories to the American soldiers. The Germans had brought them here from every corner of Europe. They had boarded trains and they had traveled for days without food or water. After they arrived, things got even worse. The Germans had herded thousands of the prisoners into execution chambers. Dachau had become a death factory, a place of wholesale, pitiless murder.

There was little need for further explanation. The evidence of a gruesome and terrible crime was everywhere to be seen.

There were forty thousand starved prisoners, and there were corpses stacked in a train near the camp. More bodies lay in front of a crematorium, used for the burning of the dead.

The conditions at Dachau were largely unknown to the outside world until the United States army liberated the camp. The same is true of conditions at similar camps in Germany and Poland. The world had long known that Adolf Hitler, the leader of Nazi Germany, despised the Jews. For more than ten years, his state persecuted the Jews by forcing them out of their homes and stealing their property. German soldiers herded the Jews into ghettos—walled-off neighborhoods that served as vast urban prisons. The German government also forced the Jews to emigrate.

After the start of World War II in 1939, Hitler's SS built dozens of death camps, including Dachau. The camps were part of what the Nazis called the Endlösung, or "Final Solution" of what they considered the Jewish "problem." Once and for all, in this vision, land under German control would be swept free of all Jews, as well as other ethnic groups, such as Gypsies, that the Nazis saw as subhuman.

The Nazis wanted to keep this mass murder of the Jews a secret. Germany did not allow any foreigners to visit the camps, with one exception. The Red Cross was allowed to visit a camp at Theresienstadt, in occupied Czechoslovakia, where the prisoners were treated more humanely.

In the meantime, escaped prisoners were telling the outside world about the camps. In countries occupied by Germany, everyone knew that German trains were bringing entire

Prisoners at Nazi concentration camps were often starved.

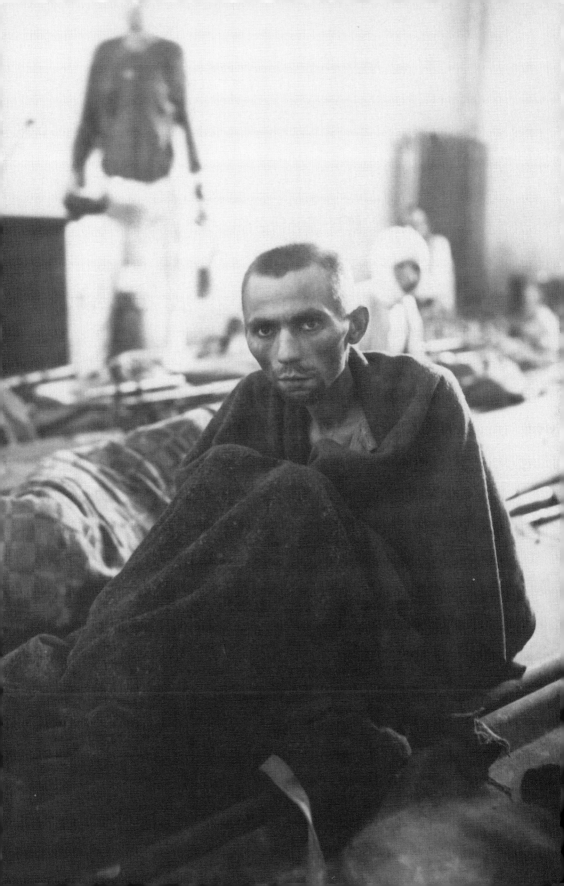

communities of Jews away from their homes. But there was a desperate war going on, a fight to the death between Germany and the rest of Europe. Few people outside Germany understood clearly what was going on at Dachau and other camps. With the defeat of Germany in the spring of 1945, the terrible truth of the "Holocaust" was seen in full detail.

A Missing Officer

Adolf Hitler committed suicide on April 30, 1945, one week before Germany's surrender. The Allied powers that defeated Germany decided that other Nazi leaders would have to pay, somehow, for Nazi war crimes and for the death camps. They decreed that these top Nazis must face a court of justice. In November 1945, twenty-one Nazi civilian ministers and military officers were put on trial for war crimes. At these trials in Nuremberg, Germany, the name of a certain SS officer—Adolf Eichmann—came up frequently.

To the Allies, Eichmann had been invisible before and during the war. He did not rank very high in the SS, the special branch of the Nazi military responsible for running the death camps. He did not command any of these camps. He did not commit any acts of violence or evict anyone from his or her home. At the Nuremberg trials, none of the accused claimed Eichmann had ordered the genocide.

Yet witness after witness at Nuremberg did name him. Eichmann, it seemed, was the engineer behind the Holocaust. He had given orders and made the necessary arrangements. In one country after another, he saw to it that Hitler's orders were carried out. Under his direction, millions of Jews were forced to ride or walk for miles to their certain death.

However, Eichmann was nowhere to be found. He had vanished, as had many SS officers, after the collapse of Nazi Germany. With a new identity and forged papers, he faded into the background, disguising himself as a laborer. When that became too difficult, he escaped from Europe, leaving his wife and three sons behind. He followed important Nazis to South America. Using the help of this network of fellow refugees, he began a new life in Argentina under the name of Ricardo Klement.

When he felt safe enough, Eichmann sent to Europe for his family. After they arrived, he moved to a desolate, nondescript suburb of Buenos Aires, the capital of Argentina. He kept to himself, raised his sons, worked at his job, and attracted little notice. He was not a rich man, but he had work and he had a family. He built his own house on a plot of land where electricity and running water were still not available. The curious eyes of neighbors could not penetrate the thick, windowless walls he raised with his own hands.

The End of an Anonymous Life

Adolf Eichmann might have considered himself lucky. He had not only survived the war, but he had also escaped the courts of justice in Europe. But Eichmann's luck began to run out in the spring of 1960. Unknown to him or to his family, the government of Israel, a Jewish nation founded after World War II, had been looking for him in Argentina for more than two years. The careless words of one of his sons had brought secret Israeli agents to Buenos Aires.

After these agents found Eichmann, they laid careful plans to capture him. They had to act in total secrecy. The government of Argentina was sympathetic to former Nazis. If it found out about the search, Eichmann might escape. An active network of Nazi refugees stood ready to warn him and give him shelter if necessary.

Even if Eichmann was captured, the Israelis would have to disguise him and get him out of Argentina—fast. If his friends or family alerted the police, the government of Argentina would surely interfere. Eichmann had become an Argentine citizen, and his kidnapping by Israeli agents would break the law. Argentina had little interest in prosecuting Nazi war criminals. Even if Eichmann was turned over to the government of Argentina, it was not certain that Argentina would put him on trial or extradite him (send him out of the country), to Israel, Germany, or anywhere else.

The search for Adolf Eichmann took place when much of the world was trying to forget World War II and Nazi Germany. In Germany itself, the Nazi party had been banned. Thousands of former Nazis and German soldiers had returned to normal civilian life. For many, the execution or imprisonment of Nazi leaders at Nuremberg had put the war and the past to rest. The majority of people were rebuilding their homes and lives. Preparing for the future seemed much more important than reliving the terrible recent past.

However, Israel, where many survivors of the Nazi genocide had escaped to, was not willing to forget or forgive. The death camps and the Final Solution had caused the deaths of 11 million people, 6 million of them Jews. For the Israeli government and for the agents pursuing Eichmann, his capture might bring some justice for this terrible crime.

Eichmann and Hitler in Austria

Adolf Eichmann was born on March 19, 1906, in the town of Solingen, in the Rhineland region of western Germany. He was the oldest child of Karl Adolf and Maria Eichmann, whose family would grow to four sons and a daughter. A middle-class family man, Karl Eichmann worked as an accountant for the Solingen Light and Power Company. In 1913, he moved to Linz, a town on the Danube River in the empire of Austria-Hungary, where he began working for the Linz Light and Power Company. Adolf Eichmann grew up in Linz and for the rest of his life considered it his hometown.

A Young Adolf Hitler

Eichmann attended elementary school until he reached the fourth grade. He then entered the Kaiser-Franz-Josef State Secondary School in Linz. A few years earlier, another middle-class student named Adolf Hitler had attended this same school. Before finishing his studies, Hitler moved to Vienna,

the capital of Austria-Hungary. For several years, he struggled to make a living as an artist. Poor and bitter at his failure, Hitler moved to Germany in 1913 to try his luck elsewhere.

Hitler and many others of his generation found a new purpose to their lives with the outbreak of World War I. The war began in the summer of 1914, after a Serbian nationalist assassinated Archduke Franz Ferdinand, the heir to the throne of Austria-Hungary. After the killing, a tangled web of treaty alliances quickly touched off a conflict across the entire continent. Germany allied itself with Austria-Hungary against the "Allies" of France, Italy, Russia, and Great Britain.

Adolf Hitler enlisted in the German army soon after the war broke out. Millions of young men were marching to the fronts in France, Italy, and Russia. For four years, the two sides battled to a bloody stalemate. While the soldiers fought from deep, muddy trenches, artillery and airplanes pounded them with shells and poison gas. Waves of soldiers raced back and forth across a "no-man's-land" in suicidal ground attacks.

In one of these battles, Adolf Hitler, who had reached the rank of corporal, was temporarily blinded by a chemical gas attack. He spent the rest of the war in a military hospital, brooding over the defeat of the German army. Hitler came to believe that Germany had been betrayed—by Socialists, Communists, liberals, Jews, and other groups he saw as traitors and outsiders. He lusted for revenge and for the day when Germany would again take its rightful place as the most feared and powerful nation in the world.

In this 1901 class photograph, Adolf Hitler is seen at the right end of top row. A few years later, Adolf Eichmann would attend the same secondary school.

A Young Adolf Eichmann

In the meantime, Adolf Eichmann, who was still too young to fight, was taking little interest in his studies and earning poor marks. Hoping to make useful social contacts for his son, Karl Eichmann had Adolf join the YMCA and the *Wandervogel*, a youth organization. Later, at the urging of a friend, Eichmann would join the *Jungfrontkampfeverband*. This group of war veterans gathered to instill patriotic ideals in the young people of Germany and Austria. Adolf Eichmann loved to join such groups and follow the guidance of strong leaders. He was a natural-born follower, who could be swayed to the opinions and the causes of men with stronger personalities.

In the fall of 1918, World War I took a disastrous turn for Germany and Austria-Hungary. Millions of German soldiers retreated from the western and eastern fronts. In November 1918, Germany asked for peace terms. An armistice was signed on November 11, 1918, in the forest of Compiègne, in northern France.

The Allies met in Paris, France, in the spring of 1919 to draw up a treaty. In June, German diplomats were summoned to Versailles, a royal palace near Paris. The victorious nations believed they had set down peace terms so severe that Germany would never again threaten war in Europe. Germany had no say in the treaty's terms. The German diplomats signed the Versailles treaty on June 28, 1919.

The Versailles treaty stripped Germany of land it had ruled in Poland and France and banned any German military units from the Rhineland, which bordered France in the west. Germany had to dismantle most of its military and pay huge reparations to the Allies for the cost of the war. The treaty doomed the Germans to many years of economic depression, unemployment, inflation, and poverty.

World War I also finished the empire of Austria-Hungary. The Habsburg monarchy, which had ruled in central Europe for seven hundred years, came to an abrupt end. Much of Austria-Hungary's territory was given to the now-independent nations of Czechoslovakia, Hungary, and Yugoslavia, as well as to Poland and Romania. Austria became a small, poor, and weak nation, the remnant of a once-powerful empire.

Adolf Eichmann, Salesman

For the Eichmanns, life went on after the end of World War I. Maria Eichmann had died during the war; Karl Eichmann remarried and bought a small mining company. Karl knew there was little hope of turning his eldest son into a professional man, such as a doctor, lawyer, or university professor. Adolf had little interest in studying or in the academic world; he was the only one in his family not to finish high school. However, Karl believed Adolf might have a future in the field of engineering. In 1921, Eichmann enrolled his son in the Linz Higher Federal College for Electrotechnology, Engineering, and Construction.

Adolf Eichmann showed little drive or ability at vocational school. When Karl saw his son struggling again, he decided that Adolf was not fit for studies of any kind. He took him out of school a last time and put him to work as an ordinary mine laborer. Soon afterward, in 1925, Adolf left his father's company to become a salesman for Oberosterreichische Elektrobau. He sold this company's radio receivers for two years, until a cousin of his stepmother pulled strings with the director of the Vacuum Oil Company. In 1927, Eichmann joined Vacuum Oil to sell gas and oil products to service stations throughout Upper Austria.

Over the next few years, Adolf Eichmann prepared to settle down and begin a family. In 1931, he was engaged to Veronika Liebl, a farmer's daughter from Czechoslovakia. The engagement lasted for several years, while Eichmann still searched for a purpose, a suitable role in life.

Eichmann began to see himself as a failure and to look at the future with apprehension.[1] When he was not traveling from one small Austrian town to another to sell Vacuum Oil products, he lived with his parents. There seemed no easy way to get ahead, and simply earning a living as a salesman did not appeal to him. But he had no wish, and no talent, for the life of an artist or writer. He had no creative impulse, and he did not want to live independently. He needed above all to follow instruction and achieve an orderly way of life.

Joining the Nazi Party

In 1932, Adolf Eichmann met Ernst Kaltenbrunner, an old friend of the family. Kaltenbrunner was a successful lawyer in Linz and a devoted follower of Adolf Hitler, the wounded German corporal. After the end of World War I, Hitler had joined the National Socialist German Workers' party, or Nazi party. Hitler quickly took control of the group and began speaking to crowds about Germany's defeat and the many humiliations of the Versailles peace treaty. In Hitler's view, the people of Germany made up a superior race of human beings who should revenge this defeat. Hitler promised to bring to account those he felt were guilty of Germany's defeat—in particular, the Jews.

Hitler believed the Jews had hatched an international conspiracy, through the war and the Versailles treaty, to bleed Germany dry. He promised that if the Nazi party should ever come to power, the "master" race of pure-blooded Germans, which he called "Aryans," would reclaim the land and money

Ernst Kaltenbrunner

Adolf Eichmann's first mentor in the Nazi party was Ernst Kaltenbrunner, an Austrian lawyer born in 1903. Kaltenbrunner joined the Nazis and the SS in 1932, a time when the party was causing a stir in the country of Adolf Hitler's birth. Kaltenbrunner was jailed for his Nazi membership in 1934 but was released in the next year. He became head of the Austrian SS at a time when the Nazi organization was still banned and operating underground.

After the annexation of Austria by Nazi Germany in 1938, Kaltenbrunner became Adolf Eichmann's boss at the Central Office for Jewish Emigration. For the Austrian Jews, such "emigration" was not voluntary. Eichmann and Kaltenbrunner stripped thousands of their possessions and forced them out of the country, under threat of imprisonment in a concentration camp if they remained.

In 1942, Kaltenbrunner succeeded Reinhard Heydrich as head of the Reichssicherheitshauptamt (RSHA, Reich Security Main Office). This office organized and supervised the systematic murder of the Jews in Nazi-occupied Europe. For his deeds during the war, Kaltenbrunner was tried as a war criminal and executed in 1946.

German troops march into Imst, Austria, after Nazi Germany took over the country in 1938.

stolen from them by their enemies. He would make Germany pure again, according to this plan, and banish the "lesser" races that in his opinion were growing like a cancer within the German nation.

Although he knew little about Hitler or Nazism, Eichmann decided to join the Nazi party. His membership, number 889,895, began on April 1, 1932. Many thousands of other men in Germany and Austria were finding the Nazi message to their liking. Like Hitler, they wanted to take part in a powerful political movement and belong to an organization with a purpose. Hannah Arendt, a philosopher who probed the mind and personality of Adolf Eichmann in her book *Eichmann in Jerusalem*, said, "From a humdrum life without significance and consequence the wind had blown him into History . . . into a Movement that always kept moving and in which somebody like him . . . could start from scratch and still make a career."[2]

Eichmann joined the *Schutzstaffel*, or SS, the same time as he joined the Nazi party and quickly rose within the SS ranks. The organization had begun as a personal bodyguard for Adolf Hitler and other party leaders. Under SS Commander Heinrich Himmler, one of Hitler's devoted comrades, the organization served as Hitler's private army. Its mission was to root out enemies of the Nazis, both in and out of the party, and enforce total obedience to the party's strictures. The job of the SS would also include persecution and destruction of the Jews, Hitler's longtime nemesis.

The Nazis Come to Power

Through the late 1920s and early 1930s, Germany struggled to recover from its defeat in World War I. Unemployment left millions of families destitute. Inflation made German currency all but worthless. Savings were wiped out, food shortages worsened, and hungry German families resorted to looting to get enough to eat. The poverty added to the bitterness many Germans felt at their nation's military humiliation. They saw their government as weak and their leaders as incapable of improving their lot. When Adolf Hitler arrived on the scene, they listened. Hitler promised to overcome the humiliations of the Versailles treaty, recover the land and honor that the nation had lost, and bring a glorious future for Germany.

In the elections of 1932, the Nazi party scored a victory that allowed it to claim more seats than any other party in the German parliament. In January 1933, the German president, Paul von Hindenburg, appointed Hitler as the nation's chancellor. In the next month, the Reichstag, the seat of the German legislature, was gutted in a fire. Although a Communist was taken into custody, some historians have speculated that the Nazis started the fire themselves. Blaming the Communists for the fire, Hitler took advantage of public outrage to strengthen his hold on power. The Nazis took complete control of the German legislature and of all government ministries. Later that year, the government banished all rival political parties, took over all of Germany's newspapers and radio stations, and established a network of police spies to watch and listen for any criticism of the new government or its policies.

The Nazis enforced rigid conformity to Hitler's ideology with the SA and the German police forces. Hundreds of suspected opponents were arrested and jailed. Many more fled the country. The Nazis also built concentration camps, including Dachau, to house those considered enemies of the state. The camps allowed the state to gather its political prisoners in one place and keep them separate from ordinary criminals.

With great thoroughness, the Nazis also went about identifying Communists, socialists, and particularly Jews— the groups Hitler blamed directly for Germany's defeat in World War I. Hitler ordered a campaign to separate the Jewish and Gentile (non-Jewish) population. Violence against the Jews went unpunished, while Nazi newspapers ran anti-Semitic articles condemning the Jews and calling for their expulsion from German society.

In Austria, meanwhile, the members of the Nazi party were stirring up trouble. The Austrian Nazis called for a greater German Reich, or empire, to include all German-speaking citizens. On June 19, 1933, the government of Austria, led by Chancellor Engelbert Dollfuss, banned the Nazi party. Dollfuss opposed Germany's anti-Semitic laws as well as the unification of Germany and Austria. Seeing Nazi Germany as a threat to Austrian independence, the nations of France, England, and Italy proclaimed, on February 17, 1934, that they would protect Austria from any invasion by Germany. These actions did not prevent the Austrian Nazis from continuing their work from underground.

Dollfuss had become a serious problem for the Nazi party in Austria. On July 25, 1934, Austrian Nazis marched into the office of the chancellor and murdered him. Their attempt to overthrow the Austrian government failed, however. Kurt von Schuschnigg succeeded Dollfuss as chancellor. Schuschnigg would soon come under intense pressure from Adolf Hitler to lift the ban on the Austrian Nazi party and allow Nazi officials into his government.

....

The Reichstag burns in February 1933.

An Uncertain Future

At the time of Hitler's rise to power, Adolf Eichmann's career with Vacuum Oil was not going well. In late 1932, the company had transferred him to Salzburg, Austria, to sell in a new, unfamiliar territory. The transfer forced him to live away from his home in Linz, and worsened his feelings of failure and aimlessness. He gradually lost all interest in his work. Early in 1933, the Vacuum Oil Company fired him.

Eichmann later would give different explanations for losing his job. To his father and to his colleagues in the Nazi party, he explained that the Jewish president of the company had fired him for his party membership. Many years later, while undergoing interrogation in Israel, he explained that business had been slow. As an unmarried man, Eichmann explained, he was the first to lose his job.

No matter who or what caused his sudden unemployment, the future looked bleak. Like Hitler, Eichmann saw better opportunities in Germany. Other members of the banned Austrian Nazi party had the same idea and crossed the German border to live as exiles. Eichmann first moved to Berlin, Germany's capital, although he remained a member of the Austrian division of the SS. The SS then transferred him to a unit stationed at Passau, on the Austrian border. He served on foot patrols through the hills of the Danube River valley. In December, Eichmann was promoted to Unterscharführer, or corporal. About the same time, Eichmann's unit at Passau was disbanded. The SS assigned him to the Deutschland battalion, a unit of Austrian party members based in the town of Dachau.

Eichmann loved the good fellowship of military life. But he also found the strict military training and routine very boring. He was not made for the life of a foot soldier. Along with the tedium of such a life came a constant uncertainty, as officers ordered him about and transferred him from post to post. Many years later, under police interrogation, Eichmann would look back on his early service in the SS, and describe it as follows: "There [at Dachau] they went in for strict military discipline; up until then, I hadn't seen anything like it . . . The company commanders were Hauptsturmführers, previously Prussian police captains. On parade, the commanders would lead their units on horseback."[3]

Eichmann was looking for an escape from the monotony of his life at Dachau when the SS transferred him back to Berlin. Instead of military duty, he found himself working as an ordinary clerk in the dusty Museum of Freemasonry. The SS had him organizing files and relics of the Masons, an international secret society that the Nazi party considered an enemy of the state.

Eichmann quickly realized that the Freemasons were not his field of interest. But while working in this museum, he encountered an officer of the SD, or Sicherheitsdienst (Security Service), a branch of the SS. The officer explained that the SD was organizing a department to deal with the Jews and the "Jewish question." Eichmann immediately volunteered himself. He joined the SD in September 1934.

The SD had been founded in 1932 by Heinrich Himmler. Under the leadership of Reinhard Heydrich, who succeeded Himmler after he was promoted, the SD served as the Nazi party's secret intelligence apparatus. It was the task of the SD to keep thorough files on Nazi party members and bring any suspected traitors or spies to justice. The SD also served as an intelligence service for the Gestapo (*Geheimestaatspolizei*), Germany's secret state police.

Enemies of the State

Soon after Hitler's appointment as chancellor in January 1933, the Nazi party made itself the sole legal political party in Germany. In February 1934, by a new Protective Custody Law, the party gave itself the authority to imprison enemies of the state in concentration camps. In the next year, new laws gave legal definition to "Aryans." By this definition, Aryans were racially "pure" members of the German nation. "Non-Aryans," those not of pure German blood, lost their civil rights.

The Nazis defined their enemies very broadly and strictly enforced their standards. Any member of any ethnic or social group considered outside the mainstream found itself in trouble with the law. Germany set up a Center for Research on Racial Hygiene, headed by Dr. Robert Ritter. It was Ritter's job to classify people according to the purity of their blood. He concentrated on the Gypsies, a nomadic people who originated in India and who lived throughout Europe in small camps. The Gypsies were interviewed, under threat of arrest, and asked about their family and ancestors. Ninety percent were classified as mixed-blood "degenerates," and the German police began moving them into prisons.

Political beliefs also condemned many Germans to persecution and arrest. Freemasons found their society banned completely. The Nazi government banned the newspapers and books of Communists and socialists. Immigrants (no matter how long their family had been living in Germany) could not be accepted within the Nazi-led society. Homosexuals were arrested and sentenced to long prison terms.

The Nazi government reserved special attention for the Jews. The Nazis defined a Jew as anyone who was married to a

Jew, had joined a Jewish religious community, had a single Jewish parent, or had at least three Jewish grandparents. On September 15, 1935, the Nuremberg Laws revoked the citizenship of all Jews within Germany. Another decree, "The Law for the Protection of German Blood and German Honor," barred marriage and sexual relations between German citizens and Jews.

Jews were already barred from schools and scientific institutes. They could not hold management positions in German companies. They could not take part in organized sports, and they found themselves losing jobs as teachers, editors, and clerks. They were subject to arrest at any time, simply for being Jewish.

Seeing a dark future in Germany, many Jews made plans to emigrate. It was not so easy to get a travel visa from a foreign country, however, and many other Jewish families felt no danger. The Jews of Germany and Europe had survived persecution before, and they would again—or so many Jews of Nazi Germany hoped. Hannah Arendt stated, "Now, the Jews felt, they had received laws of their own and would no longer be outlawed. If they kept to themselves . . . they would be able to live unmolested."[4]

At the same time as it was passing new laws against the Jews, Nazi Germany began breaking the terms of the Versailles treaty. In defiance of the treaty, the German military again began conscripting soldiers in 1935. Germany also broke the treaty by rebuilding its navy and air force. The rearmament of Germany meant jobs for millions of factory workers, who rewarded the Nazi regime with their enthusiastic support. In March 1936, Hitler ordered his military to march into the Rhineland, the border region between Germany and France where, by the terms of Versailles, all German military personnel were forbidden.

Other leaders of Europe condemned these actions but did nothing to stop them. The horrors of World War I were still fresh in the memories of the countries that had fought it. Great Britain, France, and the United States sought to avoid another war at any cost, and even at the price of appeasing Hitler. In response, the Nazi leader took advantage of the world's timidity and reluctance to oppose him with force. He also argued for the unification of Germany and Austria and the creation of a single, German-speaking Reich, or empire. Hitler believed his "Third Reich" would prove a worthy successor to the great German empires of the past and last for a thousand years.

Expert on Judaism

In 1935, Adolf Eichmann finally married his longtime fiancée, Veronika Liebl. After many years, he finally saw a better future, a future tied closely to the success of the Nazi party. He was transferred to Berlin and to Department II 112, the Jewish Department of the SD. He bought a villa on the outskirts of the city for his young family, which soon grew to three with the birth of his son Klaus. Two more boys, Horst and Dieter, arrived in the Eichmann household in the years to come.

Veronika Eichmann provided an orderly home for her husband, but she took no interest in politics. She followed the Nazi ideals for women—whose most important responsibilities, in the traditional view, were summed up in the German phrase, "Kinder, Küche, Kirche" ("children, kitchen, church"). While Adolf Eichmann found himself transferred from office to office, she remained at home, faithfully tending to their sons and supporting her husband in everything he did.

At Department II 112 of the SD, Eichmann's first assignment was to read and review *The Jewish State*, a book written by Theodore Herzl, the founder of Zionism. This movement had as its goal the founding of a Jewish state in Palestine (modern Israel) as a homeland for Jews from all over the world. For the Zionists, the city of Jerusalem, the capital of Palestine, represented the true home of the Jews and the heart and soul of their faith.

Palestine had been ruled by the British since the end of World War I. By the Balfour Declaration of 1917, Britain had promised the Jews a future homeland in Palestine. For their part, the Nazis found in Zionism a way to achieve Hitler's long-sought goal of making Germany Judenfrei, or "free of Jews." Jewish Zionists within Germany were gaining strength over those Jews who sought to assimilate in German society. Donations to Zionist organizations were rising, and Zionists found themselves treated well by Nazi officials.

The Nazis understood and approved of the Zionist outlook: The Jews made up a single nation, one persecuted throughout history, and for their survival they must establish their own state. One Nazi thinker, Johann von Leers, explained his support for an independent Jewish state:

> The fundamental idea of the Zionists to organize the Jews as a nation among nations in their own land is sound and justified, as long as it is not connected with any plan for world domination . . . If Israel takes up the plough, the hoe and the scythe and is no longer intent on making other nations its servants . . . it will find friends where before it only found enemies, and Israel and its neighbors will greet each other across freshly ploughed fields.[5]

Eichmann and many other Nazis saw the mass emigration of German Jews as the best solution for the "Jewish question." Eichmann read books on Jewish history and culture and tried to teach himself Hebrew, the ancient language of the Jews. He gave presentations on Zionism and wrote several articles and pamphlets himself. He made sure that every book or article on the subject of the Jews and Palestine passed across his desk for his study.

Eichmann had found his niche in the SD: Jewish expert. With Hitler's fanatical hatred of the Jews, he felt confident that such expertise brought him good prospects. With his obedience and diligence, and his new status as a hardworking family man, Eichmann now had a promising future in the ranks of the SS, the loyal instrument of the Nazi party.

In the Service of
the Nazi Party

The Nazi party and the SS sought to rid Germany of its Jewish population altogether. In the 1930s, simply deporting the Jews to Palestine seemed the best way to reach this goal. But the British were governing Palestine at this time. The British authorities carefully controlled immigration to avoid conflict between the Jews and the Muslim Arabs. The Arabs, like the Jews, saw Jerusalem as a holy city, and Arab families had been living in Palestine for centuries. Arab and Jewish militias were already fighting over land in Palestine. New Jewish settlers, the British believed, would make Palestine a scene of bloodshed and violence, a place difficult to control.

Nevertheless, Adolf Eichmann and other Nazi officials met with Zionist leaders from Palestine to plan the emigration of Jews from Germany. In the summer of 1937, Eichmann met an official of the Jewish militia known as the Haganah in Berlin. After a second meeting, Eichmann was invited to

Palestine, to see for himself the conditions there. Reinhard Heydrich, the leader of the SD, ordered Eichmann to travel under a false name and identity, in order not to raise British suspicions.

The orders for Eichmann's voyage came down on July 1, 1937, but the journey did not begin until November. Eichmann planned to visit Palestine as well as Egypt, which was then another colony of the British. He posed as the editor of the newspaper *Berliner Tageblatt* (a companion, Oberscharführer Herbert Hagen, posed as a student). This newspaper had been owned and edited by Jews before the Nazi government had seized control of it. Eichmann's disguise was meant to fool the British authorities in Palestine into assuming he was a Jew and allowing him to move about freely for as long as he wished.

Eichmann and Hagen took trains through Poland and as far as Constanza, Romania. They then boarded a steamship for Palestine, where the boat anchored in the port of Haifa. During the stopover, Eichmann and Hagen traveled by taxi to the slopes of Mount Carmel. They visited a Jewish kibbutz, or collective farm, and Sarona, a small colony of German Freemasons.

Eichmann and Hagen then traveled to Egypt, where they visited Alexandria and Cairo. Eichmann met Haj Amin al-Husseini who, as the grand mufti of Jerusalem, served as the leader of Palestine's Muslim Arab community. Al-Husseini and Eichmann found they both shared a strong dislike of the Jews and that both wanted to see the Jews expelled from their presence. Al-Husseini, however, could not accept the Zionist plan for emigration of the Jews to Palestine. In his opinion, Palestine should always remain the exclusive domain of the Arabs.

Eichmann and Hagen applied for a visa for a longer stay in Palestine. By this time, the British authorities knew who they were. The British had no interest in allowing Nazi party members to roam through Palestine under false identities. They knew that the DNB, or *Deutsches Nachrichtenbureau* (German News Bureau), often employed SD members posing as journalists as spies in foreign countries. They refused Eichmann's visa request. With no grounds to challenge this decision, Eichmann and Hagen soon returned to Germany.

Eichmann made a full report to Reinhard Heydrich on his return. He claimed that German Jews were frustrated in Palestine and that many of them sought to return to Germany. Eichmann also reported that the Jews were incapable of managing their own affairs. As described in his report, he felt that they were cheaters and liars who could not cooperate without Aryans in control: "This financial chaos is attributed to the fact that the Jews swindle one another . . . in Jerusalem alone there are said to be forty Jewish banks, which live by cheating their fellow Jews."[1]

Eichmann's trip to Palestine had achieved very little. However, he could now claim that he knew as much about the "Jewish question" as any man in the Nazi party. He had read the books of the Zionists, he had studied Hebrew, and he had been to Palestine to see the conditions firsthand. In the future, the leaders of the SS and SD would turn to Eichmann, their self-styled expert on the Jews, whenever they sought to put their plans for the Jews into effect.

After the Anschluss

Through the early years of his reign, Adolf Hitler often denied that he sought to annex Austria to Germany. But in his speeches, Hitler promised to create a unified Reich that would include all those of "Aryan," or pure German blood.

Reinhard Heydrich

It was Reinhard Heydrich who was responsible for setting up Nazi Germany's vast death-camp system. As Eichmann's boss in the SD, Heydrich gave Eichmann orders. In turn, Eichmann worked to make a success of Heydrich's murderous plans and visions.

Born in 1904, Heydrich became a German naval officer in the 1920s. When the Nazi party came to power, Heydrich organized the SD and also, for a time, was chief of the Gestapo. He had no qualms about ordering violence against the Jews. He had no interest in their emigration from Germany, Austria, or Europe. From the beginning, he was determined to murder as many as he possibly could. In the early years of World War II in Europe, he blocked the escape of Jews from western Europe and controlled the Einsatzgruppen squads that murdered thousands in Poland and Russia. In 1942, he laid out plans for the Final Solution at the Wannsee Conference.

Heydrich also served as governor of occupied Bohemia and Moravia. On May 27, 1942, two Czech men threw a bomb into the front seat of Heydrich's car, seriously wounding him. He died of his injuries on June 4. The Nazis carried out brutal reprisals against the Czechs for the assassination. In honor of the dead man, the SS named the genocide against the Jews in Poland "Operation Reinhard."

He believed the other countries of Europe wanted to avoid war at all costs. On March 12, 1938, Hitler ordered his army to cross the Austrian border. Nazi Germany overthrew the Austrian government and made Austria a province of greater Germany. Britain, France, and the United States protested but took no action.

Despite Hitler's promises, the Anschluss ("annexation") of Austria had been a long-sought goal of the Nazi leader. The Nazis meant not only to seize Austria, but also to destroy all of their enemies within that country. To carry this out, Einsatzgruppen, or special action squads, arrived to track down and arrest Communists, Socialists, and all those who had opposed the Anschluss.

There was also a large Austrian Jewish population to deal with. Adolf Eichmann's reputation as an expert on Jewish affairs earned him an appointment as a referent, or special officer, for Zionist affairs. Reinhard Heydrich decided on Eichmann as the man for the large and difficult task at hand. Four days after the Anschluss, Eichmann arrived in Austria to organize the persecution of the Jews in Vienna, the capital of Austria.

In the words of Hannah Arendt, Adolf Eichmann had some special qualities that made him a suitable man for this assignment: ". . . here Eichmann, for the first time in his life, discovered in himself some special qualities. There were two things he could do well, better than others: he could organize and he could negotiate."[2]

According to statements he made much later, Eichmann did not feel any prejudice against the Jews. He did not personally hate the Jews, but like many others of his time and place, he may have seen them as outsiders, and not proper German citizens.[3] The anti-Semitic ideas of Hitler and his followers did not keep him from working among them. And he had no problem acting against the Jews, if doing so would serve his own interests.

In Vienna, Eichmann set up the Central Office for Jewish Emigration in the mansion of the Jewish banker Louis von Rothschild. He summoned leaders of the local Jewish community, many of whom were already living in jails and concentration camps. Eichmann gave these men directions and gave strict rules on how the Jews could live and move about. He applied pressure and threats to keep them obedient to the wishes of the Nazi party in Germany. To back up his threats, Eichmann sent Gestapo officers and troops into Jewish neighborhoods to drag men and women from their homes, beat rabbis and other Jewish community leaders, pillage businesses and synagogues (Jewish houses of worship), and commit random murders.

Eichmann's orders were to drive all Austrian Jews from their homes. To carry this out, he had brought lists of Jewish residents. The SS had prepared these lists in Berlin well in advance of the Anschluss. Working with his committee of Jewish leaders, Eichmann set up a bureaucratic assembly line, meant to carry Austria's Jews out of the country permanently. The system stripped the Jews of their property, self-respect, and hopes. It allowed them a bit of money, which had been donated by Zionist leaders and other Jewish groups from foreign countries. Gideon Hausner, a man who would deal with Eichmann in later years, said:

> A Jew would enter the [emigration] office and he was still somebody, having a job or a shop, an apartment to live in, some property or cash in the bank, his child still registered at school. As he proceeded from window to window he was stripped of these things one by one. When he finally left the building he was jobless, his

property had been requisitioned, his child crossed off the school roll, and his passport taken away.[4]

For Adolf Eichmann and the SS, the Anschluss was an opportunity to train for much larger operations in the future. Hitler had declared that the German nation must conquer new lebensraum, or living space, in countries east of Germany. As Eichmann knew, this would mean moving the native populations out of the way and eliminating the Jews entirely. Meanwhile, the SS rewarded him for his thorough work in Austria by promoting him to *untersturmführer* (second lieutenant) in August 1938.

A Plan for Madagascar

After the Anschluss, the Nazi government passed new laws for Jews still living within the Reich. All Jewish families with property worth more than five thousand reichsmarks had to declare their goods and money as well as any jewelry they owned. Jewish shop owners also had to identify themselves as Jews on their store windows. The police and SS enforced the new laws, while the authorities ignored vandalism against Jewish property and assaults against Jews. Jews began leaving Hitler's Reich by the thousands—many of them, involuntarily. On October 27, 1938, the German government expelled fifteen thousand Jews from eastern Germany into Poland.

The relentless anti-Semitic march of the Nazis terrified the Jews of neighboring countries, who saw their turn coming. In Paris, the young Polish Jew Herschel Grynszpan felt a frenzy of despair when he heard that his family had been forced from their home in Germany to Poland. Grynszpan walked to the German embassy in Paris, demanded to see the German diplomat Ernst vom Rath, and immediately shot vom Rath, who died of his wounds on November 9. German newspapers blamed the assassination on an international Jewish conspiracy. German leaders let it be known that the time had come for war against the Jews.

For the Nazi party, November 9 was an important day, the anniversary of Hitler's failed coup attempt against the German government in 1923. Seeing an opportunity to strike at the Jews, Hitler ordered thousands of them to be arrested. The police were not to interfere in any anti-Jewish violence. That evening, the Nazi propaganda minister, Josef Goebbels, made a speech to the nation and called for vengeance for Vom Rath's murder.

Immediately, riots broke out all over Germany, with mobs attacking Jewish homes and businesses. Hundreds of homes, shops, and synagogues were destroyed. The breaking of shop windows by the thousands during this Kristallnacht ("night of broken glass") left shattered glass all over the sidewalks in Germany. The police and the Nazi party arrested twenty thousand Jews and sent them to concentration camps. Later, the Nazis released many of these Jews from the detention camps, to serve as examples to the rest that they must leave Germany or suffer the consequences.

Hitler ordered Jews to pay for the cleanup of the damage. The police closed down and seized thousands of Jewish businesses, turning them over to "Aryans." Soon afterward, the Nazi government gave the governors of German states permission to ban Jews from their public streets at certain

The funeral procession for German diplomat Ernst vom Rath is greeted by Germans giving the Nazi salute. The murder of Vom Rath inspired the Kristallnacht rampage that left Jewish businesses and synagogues in shambles.

times of day, as they saw fit. All over Germany, Jews were barred from public facilities such as parks and swimming pools. They were also barred from driving their own vehicles.

In the meantime, Nazi officials considered a plan for the mass deportation of Jews to the island of Madagascar, off the southeastern coast of Africa. In late 1938, Hitler sent an envoy named Hjalmar Schacht to London to discuss the Madagascar Plan with a British minister for refugees, George Rublee. Schacht proposed that Jewish bankers should finance the emigration of one hundred fifty thousand German Jews to Madagascar. The bankers would loan 1.5 billion marks to the German government, which would repay the loan by selling off confiscated property of the Jewish emigrants.

The Anschluss and Hitler's promise to seize more territory in Europe had inspired mistrust in the British government. Another war in Europe loomed, with the only uncertainty how, and when, such a war would begin. The Madagascar Plan needed cooperation, but cooperation between Britain and Germany was now impossible. The plan came to nothing—but it was not forgotten by Adolf Eichmann.

The Conquest of Czechoslovakia

Adolf Eichmann had moved his family to Vienna, where he had settled in as the director of "Jewish affairs." Eichmann took a practical view of his work. He attended to the details of processing Jews out of the country as efficiently as possible. His talent lay in organization, and Eichmann's office in Austria became a model all over the Third Reich. The Nazi regime appointed "Jewish experts" (*Judenreferat*) to every department in its civil government, police, and military. The job of the Judenreferat was to enforce the laws regarding Jews and obey directives concerning the Jews that came down from their bosses. Eichmann's success made him the favorite Judenreferat of Reinhard Heydrich, the leader of the SD. In February 1939, as a reward for his good work in Austria, Eichmann was promoted to *obersturmführer*, or first lieutenant.

In the meantime, Adolf Hitler was making demands on Czechoslovakia, a small neighboring country. Czechoslovakia's western region, known as the Sudetenland, held a German-speaking majority. Hitler demanded that Czechoslovakia give up the Sudetenland, which he wanted to annex to the Reich. To avoid war with Germany, Great Britain and France made an agreement with Hitler at the southern German city of Munich. The Munich agreement ceded parts of western Czechoslovakia to Germany. The agreement also guaranteed the independence of the rest of the country. Britain and France promised that if Hitler were to occupy any more countries, they would retaliate with military action.

Hitler had no intention of honoring this agreement, however. His military was now strong enough, he believed, to deal with any threat of war from Britain or France. In March 1939, he ordered his troops to occupy Bohemia and Moravia, provinces that made up two thirds of Czechoslovakia. The easternmost province, Slovakia, remained independent, but its government closely allied itself to Nazi Germany.

After German troops invaded the Czech provinces, Germany established a protectorate. This new government took orders directly from the Nazi leaders in Berlin. After this event, the SS called on its leading Jewish expert, Adolf Eichmann. Under orders from Reinhard Heydrich, Eichmann moved to the Czech capital of Prague, where he opened another office for Jewish emigration, to be modeled on the successful Vienna office.

Eichmann was not happy to leave Vienna, where he had established a successful operation, and begin anew in Prague. He felt great pride in his accomplishments in Vienna. More than two hundred thousand Jews had left the country, with the German government seizing most of their possessions, homes, and money. Years later, Eichmann would claim that he had actually been doing what was best for the Jewish community: "I had no difficulty with the Jewish functionaries. And I don't think any of them would have complained about me . . . they knew I wasn't a Jew-hater. I've never been an anti-Semite, and I've never made a secret of the fact."[5]

But Eichmann always obeyed orders. He was convinced that Jews and non-Jews could not and should not live together. Eichmann also believed in the policy of forced emigration and enthusiastically carried it out. He did not worry about the trouble and chaos this caused or the suffering of uprooted Jewish families that had lived in Germany for many generations.

There were many new challenges to overcome, however. In other nations of eastern Europe, such as Poland and Romania, anti-Semitism ran nearly as high as under the regime of Adolf Hitler. As a result, thousands of Jews were fleeing to new homes in other parts of Europe or to Palestine, where the British still maintained strict quotas for the new arrivals. It grew increasingly difficult for Eichmann to deal with the Jews under his authority and force them out of Nazi-controlled

A Czech woman weeps as she is forced to salute her Nazi occupiers.

45

territory. Eichmann began to see that a very different solution had to be found for the "Jewish question."

Eichmann's stay in Prague would be brief. His expertise in the matter of Jewish emigration made him too valuable to spend his time in the small protectorate. In the summer of 1939, he would be called to Berlin to head the Jewish office of the Gestapo, the German secret state police.

Preparing for the Final Solution

In August 1939, German officials met with leaders of the Soviet Union. Hitler had long been a determined enemy of communism, and the communist Soviet government had criticized the actions and ideology of the Nazi regime. But the two leaders did agree on the idea of dividing Poland between them. Hitler and Joseph Stalin, the Soviet leader, signed a treaty of cooperation and nonaggression. They signed another secret agreement to conquer Poland by military force. The eastern regions would go to the Soviet Union. Western Poland would be annexed by Germany.

On September 1, 1939, Germany invaded Poland. Britain, France, and Poland had signed an agreement as well, which obligated the western European powers to come to Poland's defense in case of any aggression by Germany. To honor this agreement, Britain and France immediately declared war on Germany. The invasion of Poland marked the start of World War II in Europe.

However, Britain and France could do little to stop the conquest of Poland, and the Polish military was no match for Germany's rebuilt army and air force. Within weeks, the Germans had reached Warsaw, the Polish capital, and utterly defeated the obsolete and poorly equipped army opposing them. Germany annexed western Poland, making it part of the Reich. In the meantime, Soviet armies rolled through eastern Poland. This left a small region of occupied central Poland, which Germany named the General Government. The General Government was not part of the Reich, but it was under the direct control of Nazi German officials. Germany treated it as a colony and policed it with officers and troops of the SS. Hitler appointed Hans Frank, a loyal Nazi underling, to rule the General Government.

The German drive for lebensraum in eastern Europe had continued, this time by open warfare. But the nations to the east of Germany—Poland, the Baltic countries of Latvia, Lithuania, and Estonia, as well as Ukraine and Belorussia—were also home to the largest population of Jews in Europe. Hitler's plan of conquest for these nations also created a major problem: how to deal with eastern European Jews.

Now that war had begun, all traditional channels of emigration for Jewish civilians began to close. The declared enemies of Germany would not permit new immigration across their borders. Nor would the British government allow Germany to deport Jews to Palestine. A new solution to the problem was needed by the SD commander, Reinhard Heydrich, and his subordinate, Adolf Eichmann.

The Jewish Ghettos of Poland

Three weeks after the invasion of Poland, Heydrich sent orders down to newly forming Einsatzgruppen units. These squads were made up of about three thousand officers and men. They worked independently of the German army, following the German troops into occupied territory and dealing with "enemies of the state," in particular Polish Jews. The Einsatzgruppen officers set up headquarters in larger Polish cities such as Warsaw, Krakow, and Lublin. They herded the Jews of these cities into ghettos. A ghetto was a small area of the city where the Jews were forced to live. These ghettos were frequently walled up and the living conditions were cramped. Many ghetto residents struggled to survive.

The SS officers ordered their men to act without mercy. They saw calm in the face of misery and brutality, held violence as a virtue, and instilled this quality in their followers. They knew that men ordered to assault and murder defenseless civilians had to lose all sympathy for fellow human beings. They succeeded in achieving this by using Hitler's anti-Semitic ideology. Members of the Einsatzgruppen, like Hitler, saw the Jews as less than human. They had no scruples about killing any Jews who offered resistance, or simply to serve as examples to the rest.

The Polish ghettos were surrounded by walls and barbed-wire fences. Within the ghettos, Jewish Councils (Judenrat) were set up, through which the Nazis would pass orders to the inhabitants. SS guards posted at the entrances prevented Jews from leaving, even for ordinary tasks such as going to work or shopping for food. Merchants from outside the ghettos were not permitted in, and any Jew found outside the ghetto without permission or walking the streets after the nighttime curfew was subject to immediate execution. The SS also controlled the supply of food, allowing just enough into the ghettos to prevent starvation.

The Einsatzgruppen had little trouble finding and arresting their victims. Most Jews within Poland lived in neighborhoods largely separated from the Gentile population. In addition, most Polish Gentiles were willing to cooperate with the Germans by denouncing Jews and helping the German troops roust the Jews from their hiding places. Jews resisting arrest were immediately shot.

For the Nazis, the purpose of the ghettos was to control the movement of Jews and to serve as dumping grounds for Jews from areas now governed directly by Germany. With no access to medical treatment, a very limited supply of food, and no means of making a living, the Jews of the Polish ghettos lived a desperate existence.

In the city of Lodz—which fell just one week after the German offensive began—the Germans set up one of the largest Jewish ghettos in Poland. Lodz was home to a Jewish community second only to that of Warsaw in all of Europe. On November 7, 1939, the Nazis officially incorporated the city into Germany and changed its name to Litzmannstadt, in honor of a German officer and hero of World War I. On November 16, the Jews of Lodz were forced to begin wearing an armband to identify themselves. In the next month, the German governor set out an area of 2.7 square miles (4.3 square kilometers), where more than two hundred thousand Jews were forced to live without adequate food, water, or sanitation. There they would slowly starve to death or fall victim to contagious diseases. In the meantime, an office under the leadership of Adolf Eichmann prepared to send them to their deaths.

The Nisko Plan

After the conquest of Poland, the German government organized the Head Office of Reich Security (*Reichssicherheitshauptamt*, or RSHA). This office combined the SD and the Gestapo. In October, orders went out to Adolf Eichmann to report to the new RSHA headquarters in Berlin. Eichmann became the head of Section IV B 4, a department of Section IV (the Gestapo) responsible for Jewish emigration. It was now Eichmann's task to drive the Jews out of Germany. The destination of these Jews, according to the orders of Reinhard Heydrich, would be the General Government region, located in central Poland.

Adolf Eichmann sought an efficient and permanent solution to the problem of the Jews. Eichmann still believed the best way was to set up a Jewish reservation in Poland. Creating such a reservation, he knew, would help his career in the Nazi party. In September 1939, in the company of Oberführer Franz Stahlecker, he had traveled to Nisko, a district on the San River in southern Poland. Eichmann toured the region, inspecting its farms and towns, and decided that it held everything necessary for a self-sufficient community. After visiting Nisko, Eichmann drew up a plan for evacuating the Polish residents and bringing in Jewish artisans and farmers from Austria, Germany, Bohemia, and Moravia. The plan was approved, and in early October, the first order called for the evacuation of one thousand Jews to the Nisko region arrived in Vienna.

The new residents of Nisko, however, did not find a promising haven free from the persecutions of the Nazi governments. They found a desolate, poverty-stricken region with few roads, infertile soil, no raw building materials, unsanitary water, and rampant disease. Only a few thousand even made it as far as Nisko before orders came down to stop the deportations.

Eichmann was facing serious hurdles to his Nisko Plan. Governor General Hans Frank complained about the project to his superiors. Eichmann had not consulted Frank about

the Nisko project. As a committed Nazi, Frank had no desire to live among or rule over Jews. Furthermore, he knew that should the Nisko project succeed, he would get none of the credit—but he would be held responsible for any problems it caused.

Another problem was caused by the SS moving ethnic Germans into Poland, which was supposed to become a colony of Germany. Heinrich Himmler made this a top priority for the SS. He did not want the movement of Jews to interrupt the resettlement of ethnic Germans. Eichmann's plan would demand the use of trains and soldiers needed for more important duty. Himmler also listened closely to the complaints of Hans Frank, who had influence in Berlin. Soon after the first deported Jews arrived in the Nisko region, orders came down from Himmler to stop Eichmann's plan.

The Labor Camps of Odilo Globocnik

In the fall of 1939, Adolf Eichmann was searching for an efficient and sure way to separate the Jews of Poland and Germany from the general population and "concentrate" them in closed reservations or camps. He took many of his ideas for this task from SS General Odilo Globocnik, a former gauleiter (regional governor) of Austria.

After the conquest of Poland, the German government had sent Globocnik from his post in Vienna, Austria, to Lublin, Poland. In Lublin, Globocnik came up with a plan for the arrest of the Jews, the confiscation of their property, and

....

Dr. Hans Frank, governor general of Poland, reviews troops on Nazi Party day in Krakow. Frank was opposed to Eichmann's Nisko Plan.

53

finally their use as slave laborers. In 1940, Globocnik began building forced-labor camps and factories in Lublin. These became part of a new business, owned and operated by Globocnik and four partners, known as Eastern Industries. For those slave laborers who grew sick or weak or otherwise lost their usefulness, Globocnik transformed several camps—including Belzec, Sobibor, and Treblinka—into extermination centers. Himmler also ordered Globocnik to establish a new camp at Majdanek. At these camps, Jews unfit for labor service would be murdered. It fell to Adolf Eichmann, as head of Section IV B 4, to transport Globocnik's prisoners to these forced-labor camps and death factories.

In December 1939, Reinhard Heydrich ordered Section IV B 4 to begin deporting Jews from eastern territories occupied by Nazi Germany. Instead of organizing emigration with the use of forms and regulations, Eichmann began using brute military force. On February 13, 1940, Section IV B 4 organized the transportation, in freight trains, of the entire Jewish population of Stettin, in Germany proper. The trains stopped in Lublin, where guards forced the Jews to begin marching into the countryside. Without food or water, many of the deportees died during this forced march, while others were shot for straggling. The General Government of Poland was becoming a vast killing ground for the Jewish victims of the Nazis.

At the same time, within Germany proper, the Nazi government was using gas chambers for the "mercy" killing of the mentally ill. This program was named Tiergartenstrasse 4 (T-4), after the headquarters address in Berlin. In the T-4 program, the Nazis set up poison-gas chambers in mental institutions, disguising them as shower rooms. The staff members of the institutions would herd several dozen of their

Odilo Globocnik

Ethnic cleansing, forced resettlement, and genocide were the specialties of Odilo Globocnik, an SS general who, like Eichmann and Ernst Kaltenbrunner, began his career as a Nazi in Austria. Globocnik played an important role in annexation of Austria in 1938, and for his efforts was named the gauleiter (governor) of Vienna, the Austrian capital. In November 1939, he became the SS commander for Lublin, Poland. He organized labor camps for Jewish prisoners and ordered the forced resettlement of Poles, who were to make way for German-speaking colonists in the lands conquered by the German armies.

In 1942, as Nazi Germany prepared to murder the Jewish population of Europe, Globocnik became overall supervisor of the death camps in Poland. Many historians credit him with conceiving the idea of mass execution of the Jews by gas chambers.[1] Globocnik's brutal resettlements and his role in the Holocaust made him a wanted war criminal by the end of the war. In May 1945, British troops captured him in a lakeside hideout in Austria. On the same day, Globocnik committed suicide by swallowing a cyanide capsule.

patients into the rooms and then lock the doors. They opened a valve to pipe poisonous carbon monoxide gas into the rooms and suffocate their victims.

The T-4 program resulted in the deaths of tens of thousands. Despite its approval by the Nazi government, ordinary people spoke out against the program. Relatives of the victims also raised an outcry. In August 1941, the T-4 program would be stopped in Germany. The Nazi government, however, admired the gas chambers' efficiency and moved it to the concentration camps of Poland.

The Campaign in the West

In the spring of 1940, Germany unleashed a military campaign in western Europe. The German army, or Wehrmacht, invaded and occupied Belgium, the Netherlands, and northern France. This last region came under the authority of General Otto von Stulpnagel, the German military commander of Paris. Southern France was allowed some independence under a French government established at the town of Vichy. The Vichy government cooperated with the Germans, most importantly in the matter of deporting Jews from this territory to concentration camps in eastern Europe.

Eichmann and the Nazi government then revived the Madagascar Plan. On June 30, just after the surrender of France, Adolf Hitler gave his formal approval to the plan. In October, on orders from Heinrich Himmler, Eichmann organized the transport of expelled Jews from the Saarland and the Baden region, areas within Germany, to the unoccupied southern half of France. Eichmann prepared to order transport for these Jews to Madagascar from French ports on the Mediterranean.

On Eichmann's orders, the SS rousted more than six thousand Jews from their homes, allowing each one to keep

110 pounds of luggage and a hundred marks. They herded their victims onto nine trains and sent them on a journey of four days through occupied France with no food or water. Eichmann himself took personal command of this transport, accompanying the trains in an automobile. At the station of Chalons-sur-Marne, on the border between occupied and Vichy France, the trains came to their first halt.

Here Eichmann faced a serious problem, a problem that demanded an immediate solution. Like the Nazis whom they collaborated with, the Vichy authorities were anti-Semitic. They might make trouble for Eichmann for sending Jewish refugees into their territory. If the train was not allowed to proceed, Eichmann would be responsible for several thousand Jews who could neither proceed to their destination nor return to Germany.

Eichmann climbed down from his car and met with the stationmaster of Chalons-sur-Marne. He somehow convinced the man that the train was actually a German army troop transport. Eichmann's manner was serious and authoritative, and the stationmaster showed no curiosity to know the reason for German troops to be entering Vichy territory. The trains were allowed to pass, but the Jews riding them would never see Madagascar or even the coast of the Mediterranean Sea.

Despite its approval from the top of the German government, and despite Eichmann's energy and skill at organization, the Madagascar Plan would not work. Eichmann himself believed that bureaucratic interference was to blame. As he testified many years later: "You can't imagine the difficulties I ran into, the tedious, tooth-and-nail negotiations, the thousands of objections . . . None of these people understood our aims or intentions . . . They had no contact, no inner contact, with the question."[2]

In fact, the failure of the Madagascar Plan was due to the fortunes of war. Although Germany had a powerful land army, the British controlled the seas and skies. The German navy could not possibly send huge convoys across the Mediterranean and along the coast of Africa. As soon as British submarines, planes, and surface ships discovered the German transports, they would attack. Such a mission would be suicide for the officers and crews. The actions in southern France and the weak state of the German navy ended any hope Eichmann had of transporting evacuated Jews to Madagascar.

The Invasion of the Soviet Union

In the spring of 1941, Hitler ordered his armies into southeastern Europe; Bulgaria joined the Axis powers in March 1941. In the following month, Germany attacked Yugoslavia and invaded Greece. Germany occupied Greek ports to prevent a counterattack by the Allies. Hitler also planned to use Greece as a base from which he might attack and conquer Palestine. His ultimate plan was the Nazi conquest of British and French colonies in the Middle East and control of the region's valuable oil supplies.

For a year, Hitler had been laying plans for the invasion of the Soviet Union. He had not signed the Nazi-Soviet treaty of August 1939, in order, as he announced to the world, to make peace with the Soviet government. Instead, Hitler intended to simply buy time and to carry out the conquest of western Europe with no trouble on his eastern front. In any

Heinrich Himmler (at left, in foreground) stares at a Soviet prisoner of war in a camp in Russia.

case, there was little the Soviet Union could do to prevent the conquest of France, the Netherlands, Belgium, Denmark, and Norway. Supported by the fighter-bombers of the Luftwaffe, the German air force, the Nazi armies staged a blitzkrieg, or "lightning war." The armies moved with lightning-like swiftness, with powerful mobile units of tanks and supporting infantry that moved through enemy terrain with little resistance.

After the conquest of western Europe, Germany began massing its armies on the eastern border with the Soviet Union. In June 1941, Adolf Hitler ordered the invasion, code-naming it "Operation Barbarossa." The attack caught Soviet leader Joseph Stalin and the Soviet Red Army completely by surprise. German armies moved hundreds of miles into Soviet territory while the Red Army fell back in confusion toward the capital of Moscow. Members of the Einsatzgruppen followed the regular army units into Russian territory. The four units of Einsatzgruppen were deployed as mobile killing units to carry out the mass executions of Jews, Gypsies, partisans, and Soviet officials behind the lines.

In the meantime, in Poland, the mass relocation of Jews was creating problems. There was confusion and bitter argument among the Nazi governors over where the Jews should go and who would hold responsibility for them. The invasion of the Soviet Union was also bringing millions more Jews under German control. In early 1941, Reinhard Heydrich and other Nazi leaders had been planning to make the western reaches of the Soviet Union their new Jewish reservation. The Jews of Poland, Germany, and conquered western Europe would be sent east, according to this plan, while Poland would become a territory reserved for ethnic Germans. Once Operation Barbarossa was under way, however, the Wehrmacht was making greater demands on Germany's rail transportation system. It soon became obvious that Germany would have great difficulty moving and transplanting millions of European Jews to conquered Soviet territory.

Eichmann's New Solution

According to Nazi ideas, the Jews were subhuman, unworthy of mercy or compassion in any form. If relocation and/or deportation would not work, there was only one alternative—the destruction of the Jews by genocide. In July 1941, therefore, *Reichsmarschall* Hermann Göring ordered Reinhard Heydrich to create a "Final Solution" to the problem of the Jews. Heydrich began this program on September 1, 1941, with a "Police Regulation in Regard to the Marking of Jews." This regulation required all Jews in German-occupied territory to identify themselves by wearing a badge or yellow star. The badge made it easy for German troops to arrest them at any time. On October 1, the Nazi government also passed a law forbidding all emigration from the Reich. On October 10, Heydrich and Adolf Eichmann attended a meeting in Prague where a plan for the Final Solution was discussed.

The German government began moving those who had built the poison-gas chambers within Germany to concentration camps in eastern Europe. These camps now housed thousands of Jews brought from the Polish ghettos as well as those captured by the Einsatzgruppen that had followed the German armies into Soviet territory. The camps were put under the authority of the SS; they were commanded by SS officers and received orders directly from Heinrich Himmler, the SS chief.

In the fall of 1941, Adolf Eichmann toured the General Government of Poland. He visited several camps to witness mass executions of the Jews. He experienced a ride in the cab of a gassing van, in which the engine exhaust was piped directly into a rear chamber, where trapped Jews were suffocated. At one camp, he was taken to see small, airtight buildings that served as the execution chambers. Camp guards would order their prisoners to strip naked, then herd these prisoners into the buildings and lock the doors. A large motor would be started alongside the building and the engine exhaust ventilated directly into the death chamber.

Many years later, while awaiting trial for taking part in these gruesome executions, Eichmann testified to witnessing the gassing: "I was horrified. My nerves aren't strong enough . . . I can't listen to such things . . . such things, without their affecting me. . . . I still remember how I visualized the scene and began to tremble, as if I'd been through something, some terrible experience."[3]

Many prisoners survived the first attempt at execution, while others took a long time to die. The operation was difficult, inefficient, and expensive. As Nazi leaders called for a mass murder of the Jews, pressure mounted on Eichmann and other SS officers to come up with a new method.

In August 1942, Eichmann visited Rudolf Höss, the commander at the Auschwitz camp. Höss described how he had ordered experiments on Russian prisoners of war with Zyklon-B, an insecticide used to rid the camp of lice and other insects. The prisoners were locked into a small cell, exposed to the deadly gas, and died quickly.

Eichmann and Höss decided on the use of Zyklon-B in specially built gas chambers for the mass execution of camp prisoners. Höss ordered Zyklon-B to be piped into rooms disguised as showers. The use of this poison allowed the commandants of Auschwitz and other death camps to

Haj Amin al-Husseini

Born in Jerusalem in British-held Palestine in 1893, Haj Amin al-Husseini studied at al-Azhar University in Cairo and enlisted in the Turkish army during World War I. When he returned to Palestine, he was jailed by the British in 1920 for violent rabble-rousing against the Jews. But after the death of the mufti of Jerusalem in 1921, the British pardoned him and named him as the successor and also set up a Supreme Council under al-Husseini's leadership.

Al-Husseini had one important goal: to drive the Jews from Palestine. During the 1930s, this ideal clashed with the work of Adolf Eichmann, whose specialty was emigration and deportation. However, after the start of World War II, both men contributed toward the murder of Jews.

In December 1941, Adolf Eichmann received al-Husseini in Germany. Al-Husseini had been sending telegrams of congratulations to Adolf Hitler and spoke out favorably on the Nazi persecution of the Jews. Now, with the help of Adolf Eichmann, he had the occasion to see firsthand exactly how the Nazis were accomplishing this task. Eichmann took his guest on inspection tours of the concentration camps in Poland. Al-Husseini saw in the machinery of mass execution a way to stop something he saw as a threat: the large-scale Jewish emigration to Palestine.

proceed with terrifying speed and efficiency with the killing of their prisoners. By the thousands each day, the victims of Zyklon-B were taken from the gas chambers to ovens where their bodies were burned. Höss later said that the operations at Auschwitz carried the name of the "Eichmann plan": "We discussed the details of the final solution many times . . . he showed that he was completely obsessed with the idea of destroying every single Jew he could lay his hands on."[4]

On November 9, Eichmann was promoted to *obersturm-bannführer* (major/lieutenant colonel). While Eichmann's career and importance advanced, the war was about to take a very important turn for the worse for Nazi Germany and the Axis powers. On December 7, 1941, Japan attacked American naval and air bases in the U.S. territory of Hawaii. The next day, President Franklin Roosevelt declared war on Japan. On December 11, Germany and Italy declared war on the United States. Soon, Americans would be attacking occupied Europe and the German homeland.

The Final Solution Across Europe

In January 1942, the Nazi government held a conference in Wannsee, a suburb of Berlin. The purpose of the Wannsee Conference was to complete the plans for the Final Solution. Within just a few hours, Heydrich, Eichmann, and the other officials present at the Wannsee Conference had come to an agreement. According to the minutes (written record) of the Wannsee Conference, which Adolf Eichmann prepared:

> In line with the definitive solution of the Jewish problem, the Jews will be transferred under suitable escort to the Eastern territories and there enrolled in the labor service. Formed into large labor detachments, those Jews able to work, both men and women, will work at road building as they move into these territories; it goes without saying that a large percentage of them will be eliminated by the natural death rate.
>
> The survivors—who will inevitably be those with the greatest powers of resistance—will be treated in accordance with the logic of the situation. For history

65

has shown that, once liberated, this natural elite would
embody the germ of a new Jewish revival.[1]

By this plan, Poland would become the place for the
murder of the Jews of Europe. The Nazis intended to round
them up by any means possible, herd them onto trains, and
ship them east. They intended to work them to death. Any
Jew strong enough to survive this forced labor would, after
a time, be killed.

In occupied nations, the first step in carrying this out would
be to strip the Jews of their citizenship. This would create a
population of "stateless" Jews who could not plead for legal
protection from their governments. The Jews in conquered
territories would be identified by the yellow-star badge. They
would be herded into ghettos, where possible, while the
Germans prepared their transport to concentration camps.

Eichmann's job was transportation. He was to be the
stationmaster, ordering the trains from Germany's Ministry
of Transport, directing them to cities where prisoners were
rounded up, and giving them final destinations. He took his
orders from Himmler and gave his orders to a staff of a dozen
aides and subordinates who saw that they were carried out.

Eichmann worked to make this system run as efficiently as
possible. The result was brutality and suffering for millions of
people. During a long and exhausting ride, the prisoners had
inadequate food, water, or shelter from the heat and cold.
Many of them died before reaching their destinations. When
the trains did reach the concentration camps, SS officers and
large details of guards stood waiting for them. They forced the
prisoners from the trains at gunpoint, sending the weakest
immediately to the death chambers. Those able to work were
assigned to barracks and allowed to live, temporarily.

The Germans set up several different kinds of camps for their prisoners. Concentration camps were built for holding prisoners, while labor camps were to provide workers for factories. Transit camps served as holding centers. Death camps were killing centers, although some of these also provided slave labor.

Eichmann's responsibilities made him an important part of the Final Solution. He went about his task with dedication and enthusiasm. All those who would slow or stop the deportations became his enemy. Those who helped his efforts in any way became his allies.

Assignment in Slovakia

In the spring of 1942, Eichmann traveled twice to Slovakia, once the easternmost region of Czechoslovakia. Slovakia's fascist government, headed by the Catholic priest Father Josef Tiso, supported Germany's Nazi ideology. Before the invasion of Czechoslovakia, Slovakia had promised to cooperate with Nazi Germany. As a result, Hitler had brought Bohemia and Moravia, the western and central portions of Czechoslovakia, into the Third Reich, and allowed Slovakia its independence.

Although it had allied with Nazi Germany, Slovakia would not fully cooperate with Germany in the matter of Jews. The Slovak government robbed money, property, and businesses from most of the Slovak Jews. However, Jews who had converted to Christianity before 1918 were allowed to keep their property. Slovakia set up Jewish ghettos and forced-labor camps, but refused to deport Jews out of the country.

This policy was not acceptable to Nazi Germany. In March 1942, Eichmann arrived in Bratislava, the capital of Slovakia. Using his authority as an SS officer and as a head of Section IV B 4, he persuaded the Tiso government to expel all Slovak Jews to Poland. Eichmann called the project a "resettlement."

In addition, Slovakia would have to pay five hundred reichsmarks to Germany for each deported Jew. Fearing retaliation from Germany, the Slovak government agreed. Eichmann's trains rolled from Slovakia to Poland, carrying more than fifty thousand people to the concentration camps, where most were murdered.

After June 1942, there remained thirty thousand Jews within Slovakia. Most of them were converts to Christianity, who were allowed to remain in their homeland. Eichmann's aide, Dieter Wisliceny, worked hard to persuade the Slovaks to allow the "resettlement" of all Slovakian Jews. In the meantime, Wisliceny took bribes from Jewish leaders, promising in exchange to spare the lives of individual Slovakian Jews.

By this time, the Slovak government had learned what "resettlement" really meant: imprisonment and forced labor, followed by death by shooting or in the gas chambers of Auschwitz. The Slovaks refused any further deportations from their territory. They also demanded to visit and inspect the resettlement areas for themselves.

Eichmann did not agree to this demand. In order to keep Slovakia cooperating, he had to convince Slovakian leaders that Jews were not being mistreated. He had the camp commanders in Poland force the Slovak Jews who were still alive to write letters and postcards without dates home to their relatives and friends. The messages were sent to Slovakia, while Eichmann explained to its prime minister, Vojtech Tuka, that: ". . . attention should be drawn to the postal communications of the Jews with Slovakia . . . and which, for instance, amount to more than 1000 letters and postcards for February and March this year [1942]."[2]

In the meantime, the Nazis put more pressure on Father Tiso to expel all the surviving Jews from his country. Tiso did agree to a "concentration" of the Jews in camps. However, he would still not allow the Nazis to deport these prisoners. In June 1944, Hitler would again demand that the Slovak Jews be deported, and once again Tiso refused.

At this time, the German army was retreating and the Red Army of the Soviet Union was fast approaching Slovakia. In August 1944, the Slovaks revolted against the Tiso government. Germany responded by occupying the country. The SS appeared as well, to round up and deport any Jews they could find to the death camps. By the end of the war, about three out of every four Jews of Slovakia had died at the hands of the Nazis.

Deportations in France

Eichmann's office had arranged the first roundup of Jews in occupied France in May 1941. Theodor Dannecker, Eichmann's lieutenant, was put in charge. The job was made easier by the cooperation of the Paris police force. The Parisian officers willingly allowed the deportation of foreign Jews living in France. They carried out the task peacefully by asking thousands of German, Austrian, Polish, and Czechoslovakian Jews—all of them adult men—to check in to neighborhood police stations. The men were immediately arrested and brought to new camps built at Beaune-la-Rolande and Pithiviers, to the south of the city.

About half of the Jews living in France at this time had immigrated from other countries in Europe to escape Nazi persecution. While the French authorities cooperated with the Nazis in the deportation of these foreign-born Jews, they resisted the deportation of their native Jewish citizens. For Eichmann and the SS, however, there was no difference between foreign-born and native-born Jews. The Nazis were determined to rid their territory of all Jews, no matter their homeland or birthplace. As in Slovakia, they called this action "resettlement," to hide the fact that deported Jews were being sent to death camps.

In the fall of 1942, Eichmann began organizing the deportation of native-born Jews from France. By this time, however, rumors had reached France about the true nature of this "resettlement." French officials refused to cooperate any further. The SS gave up in frustration while thousands of French Jews went into hiding or escaped to safe zones such as neutral Switzerland. Many Jews also fled to the parts of southeastern France occupied by Italy, where the Italian government refused to do any more than keep the Jews in temporary camps.

In August 1943, one roundup brought seven thousand Jewish men, women, and children to a camp at Drancy. After five days, the adults were taken away in trains to Auschwitz. After waiting ten days, Eichmann then arranged for a train for their children to the same destination. In the meantime, the children of Drancy experienced hunger, thirst, and fear. Georges Wellers, a witness of Drancy who testified at the trial of Adolf Eichmann, said,

> These children arrived at Drancy after already having been completely neglected for two or three weeks . . . they arrived with dirty, torn clothes in a very bad condition, often without buttons, often with one of their shoes completely missing, with sores on their bodies . . . At night they were completely alone in these large rooms lit by a single bulb covered in blue paint, because it was wartime and in Paris the air-raid precautions required all visible bulbs to be painted blue. They were thus in semi-darkness, more than semi-darkness; in a place which was hardly lit at all. They slept on the

floor, one next to the other. Very often they cried, they became agitated; they called for their mothers. It happened a number of times that a whole roomful of 120 children woke up in the middle of the night; they completely lost control of themselves, they screamed and woke the other rooms. It was frightful![3]

The Final Solution in the Balkans

The German invasion of the Balkan Peninsula brought Eichmann's operations to this region of southeastern Europe. There was a large population of Jews in Romania, Yugoslavia, Bulgaria, and Greece. However, not all of the nations in the Balkans cooperated in the destruction of the Jews. Bulgaria, which had allied with Nazi Germany, passed a law in January 1941 that allowed Jews who converted to Christianity freedom from anti-Semitic laws and regulations. This was different from the laws passed in Germany, where Jews were considered a separate and foreign "race" and could not change their race by going through a Christian baptism.

For Eichmann and the SS, the laws passed by the Bulgarian legislature represented defiance of Germany. In early 1942, Eichmann declared to the German Foreign Office that he had prepared facilities to receive deported Bulgarian Jews. He told the German ambassador in Bulgaria, Adolf Beckerle, to apply pressure on the Bulgarian leaders. He also sent Theodor Dannecker from France to Sofia, the capital of Bulgaria, to carry out the roundup and deportation of the Jews.

Dannecker convinced the Bulgarian government to introduce the yellow star to identify the Jews. Much to his dismay, the badge seemed only to inspire sympathy from the general population. When the Bulgarian government dropped the requirement that all Jews wear the yellow star, it also passed a law forcing the Jews to leave Sofia and live in the countryside. This new law ran directly counter to Eichmann's wishes and allowed the Bulgarian Jews to find hiding places in the countryside. Many of them lived out the war as refugees in their own country.

Germany had demanded that Croatia, where a puppet government had been set up after a German invasion, rid itself of its entire Jewish population by February 1942. The government of Croatia obliged by sending members of the Ustashe, or Croat fascist militia, into Jewish neighborhoods to carry out the roundups. The Jews were forced aboard freight trains while the government of Croatia paid Germany thirty marks for each individual sent out of the country. The houses, money, and property of the deported Jews were confiscated. In Serbia, a neighboring country, Jews were rounded up and killed as suspected partisans by regular German army units, while women and children were executed in gas vans operated by the SD.

Romania sided with Nazi Germany and, in the summer of 1941, had provided an army for the invasion of the Soviet Union. Anti-Semitism had a long history in Romania, and the Romanian government cooperated with Nazi Germany by stripping its Jews of their citizenship and carrying out mass executions of its own. Historian Hannah Arendt states that Romania would outdo even Nazi Germany in its sadistic treatment of its Jewish population: "Deportation Rumanian style consisted in herding five thousand people into freight cars and letting them die there of suffocation while the train traveled through the countryside without plan or aim for days on end . . . "[4]

In the spring of 1942, the Romanian leader Marshal Ion Antonescu asked to ship more than one hundred thousand Jews into German-occupied territory adjacent to Romania.

The Jews would be turned loose, hunted like animals, and shot down in cold blood. Eichmann himself protested this plan, which in his opinion was an inefficient method of killing. Sending so many Jews at once anyplace would certainly lead to chaos, confusion, and—even worse—the escape of many intended victims into the countryside. To avoid such problems, Eichmann arranged for the regular transport of Romanian Jews to the death camps in Poland.

As Antonescu and Eichmann planned for the killing of the Jews—each in his own way—the corrupt Romanian government arranged for simple bribery. Romanian government officials accepted money in return for granting Jews the right to leave the country. The mass executions and deportations from Romanian territory eventually stopped. As a result of the blood money paid to Antonescu's government, many Romanian Jews survived the war and eventually emigrated to Palestine.

In the matter of the Jews, Eichmann did meet with success in northern Greece. In February 1943, Eichmann sent Dieter Wisliceny to Greece to carry out deportations of the Jews from Thessalonica. This port city was home to the majority of the country's Jews. Wisliceny set up a Jewish Council, required the Jews of the city to wear the yellow star, then had the Jews rounded up into a ghetto near the railroad station. He allowed few exceptions. Trains rolled out of the Thessalonica station every day, bound for Auschwitz. Only a few thousand Jews managed to escape to southern Greece, a region occupied by Italy where the Italian authorities refused to cooperate in the deportations.

Failure in Denmark and Italy

Some countries openly defied the Final Solution. In these countries, the most dedicated Nazis found their threats

useless. Although Germany occupied Denmark early in the war, Eichmann's office had little success there. The government, king, and people of Denmark protested against the mistreatment of the Jews living among them. They protected native-born Jews and those who had fled to Denmark from Germany. According to Hannah Arendt: "When the Germans approached them rather cautiously about introducing the yellow badge, they were simply told that the King would be the first to wear it."[5]

The Danish government also refused to allow the Germans to touch the refugee Jewish population. The Danes claimed these refugees had lost their German citizenship and were now subject only to Danish laws.

Hitler and the SS did not give up. In September 1943, on Hitler's personal orders, Heinrich Himmler ordered a solution to the Jewish question in Denmark. SS officers and troops began raiding private homes, searching for Jews to deport. In response, Danish dock workers began rioting in Copenhagen (the capital of Denmark), destroying transport ships and interfering with the operation. The German military then decreed a state of martial law.

Much to the surprise of Himmler and Eichmann, resistance came not only from the civilian population, but also from within the ranks of the German military. General Hermann von Hannecken, the German military commander in Denmark, refused to cooperate with the raids and

With two SS officers accompanying him, Adolf Hitler salutes cheering crowds at a Nazi Party Day rally in Nuremberg, Germany. The Final Solution that Eichmann was helping carry out all over Europe was based on Hitler's beliefs of racial superiority.

deportations. Even SS commanders began protesting orders handed down from Berlin. Living among people determined to resist the Final Solution, these obedient Nazis—who had trained for years to follow Adolf Hitler and Nazi ideas without question—began resisting as well.

In order to bring cooperation, the SS then promised that all Jews deported from Denmark would be sent to the "model camp" at Theresienstadt. When even this promise failed to bring cooperation, Eichmann sent a commando unit under the command of his aide Rolf Gunther to Denmark. Gunther found that he was unable to convince Von Hannecken to obey directives from the SS. On October 1, Germany sent regular police officers into Denmark to round up any Jews they could find and bring them to transport ships anchored in the harbor of Copenhagen.

The German policemen had little success. Tipped off in advance of the operation, the vast majority of Danish Jews had gone into hiding. Most civilians hiding these Jews refused to open their doors. The Germans did not force their way in, because they were told to avoid any encounters with the Danish police.

Through the rest of October, helped by wealthy Danish citizens, about eight thousand Jews and Christians married to Jews rode fishing boats and ferries to safe harbor in unoccupied Sweden. The rest remained safely in hiding, while five hundred unlucky enough to be captured by the Germans were sent to Theresienstadt. These prisoners were helped during their captivity by gifts and money sent from Denmark; 423 of them survived the war.[6] For Adolf Eichmann, Denmark had been a complete failure.

Eichmann also found trouble in Italy, one of Nazi Germany's allies during World War II. In October 1943, as the SS was failing in Denmark, he sent Theodor Dannecker to Italy to arrange the deportation of Italian Jews to concentration camps in northern Europe.

Italy had been a member of the Axis powers, allied to Germany by its leader Benito Mussolini. Nevertheless, Italian military and civilian officials showed little enthusiasm for the Final Solution. Although they often made promises to the German commanders to round up and deport their Jews, they always found some excuse not to do so. They allowed thousands of Italian Jews to escape to safe zones outside of the country.

In the summer of 1943, Mussolini was overthrown in a coup and the fascist government of Italy fell from power. When the new Italian government declared war on Germany, Hitler responded by ordering the invasion and occupation of his former ally. After this event, Eichmann began issuing the necessary orders concerning the Jews. German troops began searching for Jews in Rome, the Italian capital, but found few of them to capture. Italian civilians had warned most Jewish families to go into hiding.

In November, the Italian government decreed that Jews captured within Italy would be allowed to remain there as prisoners in Italian concentration camps. With the army and the SS stretched thin on the battlefronts, the Nazi government and the RSHA went along. But in the next year, as Rome was about to fall to the Allies, members of the SD rounded up several thousand Jews. Eichmann arranged to ship these prisoners to Auschwitz, where the majority of them did not survive the war.

Liquidating the Ghettos

In the meantime, the SS was clearing the Polish ghettos. Eichmann's troops arrested entire neighborhoods in Warsaw,

Krakow, Lublin, Lodz, and other cities and brought them to the death camps. The task became more urgent in April 1943, when the Jews who still remained trapped in the Warsaw ghetto rose in revolt. Armed with rifles obtained from the Polish underground, the Jews of Warsaw fought back as the SS began rounding up the inhabitants for the journey to Auschwitz.

The Germans put down the Warsaw ghetto uprising with savage ruthlessness. Four months later, Eichmann and the SS began preparing to deal with Poland's second largest ghetto in the city of Lodz. Since May 1, 1940, the day the ghetto was sealed off from the surrounding city, about two hundred thirty thousand Jews of Lodz had lived with disease, overcrowding, random beatings and killings, and starvation. But the ghetto had also set up small factories, where Jewish workers produced clothing and military goods that were traded to the Germans in exchange for food.

From time to time, the Germans ordered a train to Lodz. Each of these trains took away several thousand Jews to the death camp at Chelmno. After September 1942, with German armies in Russia running short of supplies, Germany diverted the trains to the eastern front. For Adolf Eichmann, clearing the Lodz ghetto remained an important but unfinished task.

In January 1944, Eichmann went to Lodz personally to meet with Hans Biebow, the ghetto's amstleiter, or "commissioner," who controlled every aspect of the ghetto—factory production, working conditions, housing, and food rationing. Shortly afterward, Eichmann gave the order to deport more than five thousand children directly out of the ghetto to the death camps. On June 10, with Soviet armies rapidly approaching the borders of Poland, Heinrich Himmler ordered

After the Warsaw ghetto uprising was defeated by the Nazis, many residents were taken prisoner.

the Lodz ghetto cleared. Over the next few weeks, nearly every Jewish resident of Lodz disappeared to Chelmno and Auschwitz. By the end of the war, out of a quarter million residents of the Lodz ghetto, only about eight hundred remained.[7]

Acts of Mercy

Eichmann was an obedient servant of Adolf Hitler and the Nazi ideals. He believed in the Final Solution, and he ordered the deportation of millions of Jews to their certain deaths. But Adolf Eichmann also enjoyed exercising power. From time to

Hans Frank

The Nazi master of occupied Poland, Hans Frank, frequently quarreled with Eichmann and every other German leader involved with the drive for lebensraum in eastern Europe. Trained as a lawyer, he had served as a Nazi minister since 1933, the first year of Hitler's rule in Germany. In September 1939, he was named Governor General in the region of central Poland not incorporated into Germany proper.

Frank was responsible for forcing the Jews into Polish ghettos and setting up the system of Jewish slave labor, from which the Nazis and the SS profited. He maneuvered constantly for influence with Hitler and protested the movement of Jews into his state from Germany and from the east. After his capture by the Allies in May 1945, he claimed to be unaware of the death camps operating in his territory until 1944, two years after they were set up. He was tried as a war criminal and executed in October 1946.

Jews in the Polish ghettos often had to chop up their furniture for firewood.

time, he did intercede on behalf of Jews whom he knew. He considered Jewish doctors, lawyers, and professors worthy of careful handling. Sometimes, he also showed respect to members of the Jewish councils, which collaborated with the Nazis in their efforts to control the general population of cities such as Vienna, Prague, Berlin, and Budapest.

In 1944, Eichmann received a message from Rudolf Höss, the commandant of Auschwitz. Höss explained that a certain Bertold Storfer was begging to speak with Eichmann. Storfer, a member of the Vienna Jewish council, had been deported to Auschwitz for going into hiding. Eichmann, who remembered Storfer from his days in the Vienna emigration office, traveled to Auschwitz to see what he could do. By the orders of Heinrich Himmler, no one who arrived at a concentration camp as a prisoner could ever leave. Eichmann saw to it that Storfer was given the easy task of sweeping the gravel paths among the barracks and command buildings, with the right to sit down and rest whenever he wanted.

Unfortunately, even the friendship of Adolf Eichmann could not help a prisoner once he was within the gates of a place like Auschwitz. About six weeks after Eichmann left the camp, Storfer was executed by a firing squad.

In countries where Eichmann was unable to commandeer large numbers of trains and troops, he sometimes found helpful collaborators. In April 1940, Germany had invaded Norway and set up a puppet government. Vidkun Quisling, the head of a fascist, anti-Semitic political movement known as the National Union, then became the country's new Nazi-friendly leader. Unlike most Norwegians, Quisling was sympathetic to Hitler's opinions of the Jews.

Born in 1887, Quisling rose to the rank of major in the Norwegian military. He served as a diplomat and as Norway's minister of defense from 1931 to 1933. After the outbreak of World War II, Quisling paid a visit to Adolf Hitler, encouraging Hitler to occupy Norway and set up a puppet government. In his writings and speeches, Quisling also called for the deportation of all Jewish refugees who had sought shelter within Norway. Quisling and his supporters did not care how these foreign-born Jews left or what might happen to them at their final destination.

In October 1942, Adolf Eichmann began giving instructions for the roundup of the Norwegian Jews. About two thousand people were arrested and sent to temporary camps. On November 25, 1942, Eichmann ordered their evacuation to Auschwitz. However, Norway's neighbor Sweden, a neutral country in the war, immediately offered refuge to these Jewish prisoners. The Nazi government officially refused this request, but nearly half of the Jews in Norway's camps managed to cross the border to safety.

After the end of World War II in 1945, Quisling's cooperation with Eichmann and the Nazis would cost him dearly. He was branded a collaborator, tried for high treason, convicted, and executed. Since World War II, in Norway, Quisling's name has been a synonym for those who betray their country for power and personal gain.

Theresienstadt: Eichmann's Model Camp

In late 1941, Reinhard Heydrich decided that it might be useful to create a camp unlike any other—a "model camp." In such a camp, the SS could show good conditions, well-fed prisoners, and relatively easy discipline. In November 1941, orders went out to Theresienstadt, a village near the border of Germany in what is now the Czech Republic. All Czech residents had to leave by the end of May.

After that time, according to Heydrich's idea, Theresienstadt would be home only to certain categories of Jewish prisoners. Those that the SS sent to the camp were sixty-five years of age, well-known Jewish businessmen or community leaders, and those who had won medals or had suffered injury while fighting for Germany in World War I. There the prisoners lived in barracks or in the abandoned homes of the Theresienstadt villages. A Jewish council, taking orders from the SS commandant, governed them and gave them useful labor to perform.

During the war, Eichmann often used Theresienstadt as a bargaining chip when dealing with Jewish leaders. He offered them the hope of living out the war in relative safety in return for their cooperation and obedience. To hide the truth of the labor and death camps built elsewhere, the Nazis also allowed the International Red Cross into Theresienstadt for a tour of inspection. This was the first and only time they ever allowed an outside group into one of their concentration camps.

5

Eichmann in Hungary

In early 1944, the war on the eastern front against the Soviet Red Army was not going well for Germany. After reaching the outskirts of Moscow, the Soviet capital, the German army had been stopped. A defeat at the city of Stalingrad, on the Volga River, had ended with the surrender of the German Sixth Army. Brutal winter cold, a lack of ammunition and transport, and desperate counterattacks by units of the Red Army turned the tide against the Wehrmacht. The German armies began retreating through western Russia and the Ukraine.

Adolf Hitler feared that the relentless westward march of the Red Army might convince his allies in eastern Europe, including Hungary, to break with Nazi Germany. For this reason, Hitler ordered Operation Margarete, the occupation of Hungary. The invasion began on March 18, 1944.

In the weeks before this, Eichmann had been working about fifty miles east of Berlin in the village of Wuhlheide.

He had received orders to set up an alternate headquarters for the Gestapo. While making a tour of inspection at Wuhlheide, Gruppenführer Heinrich Muller, the Gestapo chief, ordered Eichmann to leave as soon as possible for Budapest, Hungary. Eichmann's new task was to carry out the Final Solution among the Hungarian Jews.

Eichmann saw Hungary as a worthy challenge. He went at his new assignment with energy and dedication. His first order was for a grand procession into Hungary. With Eichmann in the lead, several dozen civilian cars and military vehicles followed the Wehrmacht's First Armored Division across the Hungarian border. After arriving in Budapest, the Hungarian capital, Eichmann summoned his most trusted aides to his office, including Theodor Dannecker, Rolf Gunther, and Dieter Wisliceny.

Hungary was the last home to a large population of Jews in Nazi-occupied Europe. Although anti-Semitism was common in the government and in Hungarian society, the Jews of Hungary were left to go about their lives. According to author Quentin Reynolds:

> Until [the Nazi occupation] the million Jews of Hungary had enjoyed relative peace. . . . Recently rumors had reached Hungary that some five million Jews had been exterminated, but the Hungarians just did not believe it. Their attitude was, "Even if there is some basis for this rumor, it can never happen to us."[1]

Eichmann knew that Hitler greatly feared an uprising of Hungarian Jews. With Soviet armies approaching Hungary, he also knew he had little time. He invited local Jewish leaders to a meeting, where they were asked to set up a Jewish Council. The council would convey orders from Eichmann's office to the Jewish citizens of Hungary.

Eichmann's aides, in the meantime, made arrangements to receive bribes from these same Jewish leaders. Dieter Wisliceny put forth a "European Plan" to Dr. Israel Kastner and Joel Brand, leaders of Budapest's Jewish business community. By the European Plan, Jewish organizations around the world would raise money and simply ransom the Jews of Hungary. They would be kept safe from the ghettos and the deportation trains in exchange for a payment of $2 million.

Money began flowing freely into the offices of the German officials. Wisliceny and his colleagues took bribes large and small, for a variety of favors given to the Jews of Budapest. The money supported a lavish lifestyle, much improved over their lives within Germany. The German officers lived in the city's finest homes and worked out of palaces and ministries commandeered from the Hungarian government.

Eichmann allowed bribery, however, only if it helped him implement the Final Solution. He had no intention of sparing the lives of any Jews, no matter how much money they brought to his office. However, he did want their cooperation, and he won it with false assurances and by appearing to treat their leaders with respect. As a result, the members of the Jewish council offered little resistance to Eichmann's orders and regulations.

Hungary's government ministers and police force, many of whom were anti-Semitic themselves, were also part of his plan. Many of them had joined the Arrow Cross movement, an imitation of the Nazi party that carried out violence against the Jews and other minorities within Hungary. Although Germany was retreating from Russia, and it was obvious that the Nazis would lose the war, SS officers were still willing to use threats and violence to achieve their aims.

Willingly or not, the Hungarian police began rounding up Jews and forcing them at gunpoint into a Budapest ghetto. German troops raided the ghetto, arrested hundreds of Jews at a time, and marched them to the city's train stations. At gunpoint, crowds of desperate and fearful passengers boarded freight trains arranged by Eichmann's office for the journey to Auschwitz.

Jewish Lives for Trucks

Under Eichmann's direction, the deportations in Hungary in the spring of 1944 went ahead with brutal efficiency. As many as twelve thousand Hungarian Jews arrived every day at the gates of Auschwitz. Most of them were immediately sent to the gas chambers. The great crowds of prisoners put a heavy strain on the execution machinery. At times, Auschwitz commandant Rudolf Höss complained to Eichmann and asked that the trains be slowed down or stopped.

In Berlin, in the meantime, Heinrich Himmler realized that Germany was losing the war. Himmler began searching for some way to save himself by making deals with the Allies. In April 1944, Himmler hit on a macabre business offer. He would spare the lives of a million Jews, in return for certain military and civilian goods to be supplied to Germany by the Allies.

Himmler decided to make the offer through Adolf Eichmann in Hungary. Eichmann made the offer in turn to businessman Joel Brand, as reported by historian Randolph Braham:

> The one million Jews were to be delivered via Germany after the receipt of the specified goods. . . . 200 tons of tea, 800 tons of coffee, 2 million cases of soap, an unspecified quantity of tungsten and other military-related materials, and 10,000 trucks. . . . The proposal

87

further stipulated that the first installment of 100,000 Jews would be released and the Auschwitz gas chambers blown up soon after the receipt of the Allies' positive response.[2]

Eichmann allowed Joel Brand to travel to Istanbul, Turkey, to present the offer to the Allies. With this deal, Himmler believed that he might be able to conclude a separate peace with the Allies, save his own skin, and succeed Hitler as Germany's new leader. However, Brand was detained during his journey by the British in Cairo, who suspected a Nazi trick.

The Brand mission and Himmler's deal turned out a complete failure. Nevertheless, Eichmann and his staff in Budapest continued to make their own deals with the Jewish leaders in Budapest. These leaders brought money, jewelry, and other valuables to Eichmann's offices in hopes that he would spare the lives of friends and colleagues. In the summer of 1944, Eichmann blackmailed the Hungarian Jewish leaders, promising to arrest but not deport the Jews in exchange for money. He also claimed the money would help pay for food and medicine for the Jews already sent out of the country.

The bribery and promises did nothing to help the Jews of Hungary. Eichmann simply lied while accepting these bribes and business deals in order to make his assigned task as easy as possible. He never wavered in his conviction that the Jews of Europe had to be eliminated, country by country. As the war grew increasingly desperate, Eichmann worked even harder to carry out the Final Solution.

Trouble With Horthy and Wallenberg

On June 6, 1944, a huge Allied invasion force landed on the shores of Normandy, on the northern coast of France. Germany was now fighting in western and eastern Europe.

Italy was falling to the Allies, and German armies were retreating in the Balkans.

Reports of Germany's wholesale slaughter of European Jews were reaching the outside world. Neutral countries and the Catholic Church were protesting the deportations in Hungary. Allied leaders, including President Franklin Roosevelt of the United States, promised to punish the Hungarian government if they continued to collaborate with the Nazis. Miklós Horthy, the Hungarian head of government, ordered a stop to the deportations in late June.

Eichmann did his utmost to see that they continued. On July 14, 1944, Horthy heard of a shipment of fifteen hundred Jews making its way toward the border and Auschwitz. He ordered the train to turn back, demanded that Eichmann cease the deportations, and ordered his own ministers to stop cooperating with the Germans.

The train did turn back, and the Jews on board were placed in a temporary camp. But Eichmann was determined not to give in. For him, Germany was in command in Budapest, and Horthy was merely serving as a useful tool for the Final Solution. To make certain no interference would come from Budapest's Jewish leaders, he told them that, temporarily, they would not be allowed to leave. In the meantime, Eichmann sent down orders to reload the Jews in the temporary camp onto the trains, which then rushed out of Hungary in secret.

The Jewish Council of Budapest could do nothing to prevent Eichmann's maneuvers. But Eichmann did find a worthy adversary in midsummer when a Swedish diplomat, Raoul Wallenberg, arrived in Budapest. Wallenberg's mission, using the neutral Swedish embassy as cover, was to save as many Jews as possible, using any means he could think of.

Wallenberg went at his task with as much dedication and enthusiasm as did Adolf Eichmann. His plan relied on a special Schutzpass, which he designed and had printed. These passes extended the protection of the Swedish government to individuals who held them. Wallenberg also set up safe houses in Budapest under the flags of Sweden and of the International Red Cross. Jews crowded into the safe houses, where they were safe from the Nazis and the Arrow Cross. He arrived at train stations just as deportations were taking place, set up small folding tables, and granted safe conduct passes to condemned Jews on the spot. He boarded trains under the eyes of German and Arrow Cross guards, yelling for the guards to free prisoners.

Wallenberg acted in open defiance of Adolf Eichmann, whom he met several times face to face. Eichmann often made threats toward Wallenberg—all of which Wallenberg ignored.

The Forced March

On August 14, Heinrich Himmler told Eichmann to send all Jews out of Budapest to the concentration camps by August 25. Once again, Horthy resisted Eichmann's orders to the Hungarian police and insisted that the Budapest Jews be sent to Hungarian camps. Eichmann railed against Horthy's actions but found he could do nothing. He did not have enough troops of his own to carry out the deportations if the Hungarian government did not cooperate. Finding his orders ignored and his efforts blocked, Eichmann asked for permission to leave Hungary.

Eichmann made every effort within his power to deport all of Hungary's Jews to the death camps.

Raoul Wallenberg

The son of a wealthy and prestigious Swedish family, Raoul Wallenberg was in many ways the opposite of Adolf Eichmann. He was a successful student and businessman. He took no interest in politics, and he did not join political organizations. Most importantly, he was not a man who enjoyed following orders. Instead, he made his own rules and created his own solutions.

Wallenberg arrived in Hungary in the summer of 1944. His mission as first secretary of the Swedish legation was to save the surviving Jews of Hungary from Adolf Eichmann. His special passports and safe houses and his defiance of Nazi officers and troops allowed thousands of Jews to survive the brutal Nazi occupation of Hungary. Wallenberg himself was not so lucky. In January 1945, he was captured by the Soviet Red Army, brought back to the Soviet Union, accused of spying for the United States in Hungary, and imprisoned. He would spend the rest of his life in the Soviet prison system and never return to Sweden.

In the meantime, Horthy himself began negotiating with the Allies for a separate peace. When he heard of this, Adolf Hitler ordered Horthy's government to be overthrown. On October 15, 1944, Hitler ordered Horthy to appoint Ferenc Szalasi, the leader of the Arrow Cross, as the new prime minister of Hungary. Shortly after Horthy agreed to this, he was arrested and brought to Germany, where he became a prisoner of the Nazis.

On October 17, two days after Szalasi and the Arrow Cross came to power, Eichmann returned to Hungary from Berlin to resume deportations, and to face new problems. Although the Hungarian fascists were in power, the German army was commandeering trains for the movement of troops. Allied bombing raids had destroyed long sections of track, as well as railroad yards and stations, junctions, bridges, river crossings, and embankments.

One other problem arrived in the form of a direct order from Heinrich Himmler, who told Eichmann to stop the deportations of the Jews immediately. Himmler, on his own, had decided to stop the genocide. He was not acting out of mercy or compassion. The Jews were now worth more to the SS commander alive than dead. Himmler believed he might be able to negotiate his own peace with the Allies and use the surviving Jewish population as a bargaining chip.

Eichmann did not allow these conditions, or Himmler's orders, to deter him. Instead of deporting the Jews by train to Auschwitz, he began marching them out of Budapest on foot, toward Austria. He knew that a long forced march of 130 miles, with his prisoners denied adequate food and shelter, would result in many deaths. As cover, he claimed that these prisoners would be put to work building tank traps and other defenses for the battle against the invading Allies.

Eichmann ordered the Arrow Cross to begin rounding up fifty thousand Jews for the march. Any adult capable of walking and all children over the age of ten would have to take to the roads to an almost-certain death. On November 10, the forced march of the Budapest Jews began.

Six days later, a party of three German men arrived at the outskirts of Budapest in an official car. They had driven from Vienna. On their way to the city, they had passed the long columns of bedraggled, starving people—the forced marches from Budapest ordered by Adolf Eichmann. They had seen piles of corpses by the side of the road, where those who had lost the strength to continue had been shot and left to die. A Budapest Jew named Arye Breszlauer stated:

> I arrived at Hegyeshalom. I found the people in a state—I was accustomed to unpleasant sights, but it was a picture . . . there was a large farmyard there, with a big barn into which the people had been confined— thousands of them . . . They were under strict guard. I could see them— through holes in the wood, through chinks in the boards. There were also small holes. I saw faces of people who had made their way for 200–220 kilometres without food. There was the fear of death in their countenances. They were in a horrible state, without any hygienic conditions. They performed their bodily functions inside the barn. There were women and men there. I could only hear shouts of "Help!" They thought that people had come from the embassy, they believed that they were able to save them all, and they began shouting. I saw they were in an awful state. They were hungry and thirsty. I am not capable of describing the situation in which I saw these people.[3]

On November 17, an order came down to stop the marches immediately. Thousands of Jews who had set out from Budapest returned to the city. Four days later, in defiance of

Himmler's expressed wishes, Eichmann gave the order to resume the forced march.

In the meantime, Himmler was still hard at work cutting deals. He allowed a few hundred Budapest Jews, selected by Dr. Rudolf Kastner, to escape to Switzerland in exchange for money. Still in Budapest, Raoul Wallenberg was giving out safe-conduct passes to the Jews on the forced march. These papers allowed them to escape the march into a camp where they would be safe until the end of the war.

Eichmann was not finished in Budapest, however. As the Soviet armies marched ever closer to the city, he planned an all-out massacre of Jews who remained. Eichmann's orders went out to General August Schmidthuber, the commander of the SS Feldherrenhalle Division.

Raoul Wallenberg heard about the planned massacre and decided to stop it. Through an accomplice in the Arrow Cross, Pal Szalay, Wallenberg sent a message to Schmidthuber that, should the shootings take place, the Allied armies would hold him personally responsible, put him on trial, and have him executed as a war criminal. In defiance of Eichmann's orders, Schmidthuber then called off the massacre in the Budapest ghetto.

About one hundred thousand Jews remained alive within Budapest, and about one hundred twenty thousand survived in all of Hungary. Through his aides, SS troops, and the members of the Arrow Cross, Adolf Eichmann had been directly responsible for the killing of more than half a million Jewish civilians. His actions in Hungary would later make Eichmann notorious around the world, a symbol of the worst genocide in history.

6

The Defeat of Nazi Germany

In late 1944, the Soviet Red Army was advancing rapidly toward the Hungarian capital of Budapest. A few days before Christmas, Adolf Eichmann could hear shelling in the outskirts of the city. He knew that Hitler was ordering every available man to the front, and he expected to take command of a combat unit. By his own testimony, he could hardly wait: "The heavier the shelling grew and the closer the front came, the happier and calmer and more elated I became. . . . All I did was study the situation at the front and wait impatiently to be appointed military commander."[1]

Many Gestapo and SS units were already fighting alongside the battered German armies. But very different orders came for Adolf Eichmann on Christmas Eve, 1944: He was to leave Budapest immediately. Eichmann drove to Berlin, where he found a city sliding into anarchy.

Allied air raids were pounding the capital day and night. Old men and young boys were building barricades and preparing to fight in the streets. The government could not communicate with its armies in the field. Top Nazi officials were planning their escape or their surrender to the British or Americans before the Red Army reached the capital.

As the Allies approached, Eichmann helped prepare the last-ditch defenses. On orders from his superiors, he also burned orders, reports, and files kept in his office. In the meantime, his colleagues were busily preparing to change their identities and elude capture. The question on everyone's mind was: Soviets or Americans? Which army would capture the city? Nazi leaders and officers most feared surrender to the Soviets, as they believed the Red Army would show them no mercy whatsoever. This was mainly because the Soviets had suffered the most severe losses at the hands of the Germans. With the Americans, they believed they had a chance to survive the end of the war as prisoners and eventually, perhaps, return to a normal civilian life.

Commander of Hostages and Partisans

Heinrich Himmler sent orders to Eichmann to round up prominent Jewish prisoners at Theresienstadt and bring them south, to Austria. Himmler planned to negotiate the safe release of these prisoners with General Dwight Eisenhower, the overall Allied commander on the western front. Eichmann hurried out of Berlin, driving to Prague and then on to Austria.

In Austria, Eichmann found the top commanders, men who had sworn their eternal loyalty to Adolf Hitler, frantically preparing to escape into the mountains. These officers intended to fight a guerrilla war in Austria's remote forests. If that failed, they would disappear and escape to neutral Switzerland—or even farther abroad, to South America.

97

Eichmann soon forgot about his orders from Himmler. There were no other officers willing to deal with the Jews, no matter who ordered them to do so. In the resort of Altaussee, Eichmann met up once again with Ernst Kaltenbrunner, the man who had recruited him into the Nazi party. Kaltenbrunner ordered Eichmann to take command of partisans (men fighting out of uniform). His assignment was to defend a remote mountain valley known as the Totes Gebirge.

Eichmann set up a new headquarters in Rettenbachalm, a high mountain pasture, and collected a few hundred old men, young boys, and disabled men, few of whom had any military training. Soon afterward, he received fresh orders from Kaltenbrunner: On no account was anyone to fire on either British or American troops.

In the meantime, Berlin had fallen in the last week of April. The Allies were occupying Germany, and on April 30, Adolf Hitler had committed suicide. Eichmann sheltered in the mountains, safe from the advancing Allied armies. But Eichmann's notoriety made him an outcast even among his brother officers. One of his companions, Anton Burger, told Eichmann he was being hunted by the Allies as a war criminal. Eichmann left to meet his wife a final time:

> In Altaussee I gave my wife a briefcase full of pearl barley and half a sack of flour as a final present. And poison capsules, one for each child and one for my wife, and I said to her: "If the Russians come, you must bite them; if the Americans or the British come, then you needn't."

Germany's defeat left the country in ruins. This factory was devastated by Allied bombing in the spring of 1945. In the distance, outside of the factory's site, are blocks of windowless and partially unroofed workers' homes.

> That may have been at the end of April or the beginning
> of May 1945. Those were my only "provisions."[2]

Eichmann believed that the Russians would not respect civilians and that a Russian capture of Vienna would mean the murder of his family. The Americans captured Vienna, however, and Vera Eichmann and her children survived the war and its aftermath.

Eichmann, in the meantime, fled north to Germany. A few days later, near the town of Ulm, an American patrol captured him. Not aware of his identity, the patrol brought him to a nearby prisoner-of-war camp, where he was interrogated. Eichmann gave his name as Adolf Barth, claiming to be a corporal in the Luftwaffe, Nazi Germany's air force. Later, after he was moved to another camp, he changed his name to Otto Eckmann. An intense hunt for war criminals was going on, and while a prisoner of the Americans, Eichmann carefully kept his identity a secret from his captors and from fellow prisoners.

There was at least one civilian also looking for him. In Austria, a Jewish refugee named Simon Wiesenthal, who had survived years of captivity in forced-labor camps, had vowed to bring Nazi war criminals to justice. Wiesenthal knew the story of Adolf Eichmann and, while searching for his prey in Austria, came across Eichmann's parents, who claimed that their son had not come home from the war. Agents of the Counter-Intelligence Corps (CIC), an American intelligence agency, also found Eichmann's wife, Vera Liebl, in Altaussee. Liebl claimed to have divorced Eichmann in March 1945, and to have taken her maiden name again. But she offered no information about Eichmann's whereabouts to the CIC or to Wiesenthal.

The Nuremberg Trials

On their drive to Berlin in the final months of the war, the Allied armies liberated dozens of concentration camps in Germany and Poland. In these camps, they found horrifying evidence of one of the greatest crimes in history. Hollowed-eyed prisoners with emaciated bodies and ragged clothing were found wandering through the camps. In some places, naked and unburied corpses were found stacked like firewood outside of gas chambers and cremation ovens. Allied officers brought local civilians into the camps to show these sights to the German people, and in some places to force them to

Civilians of Ludwigslust, Germany, are made to view a nearby concentration camp by the United States 82nd Airborne Division on May 6, 1945.

bury the bodies. A few camps, including Auschwitz in Poland, were preserved as memorials to the millions of people who had died at the hands of the Nazis.

Journalists and historians realized they had lived in the time of a terrible genocide—the attempted murder of the entire Jewish population of Europe. Nobody could possibly know the number of victims, although by many estimates 11 million people, including about 6 million Jews, had been shot or murdered with poison gas. They would eventually give this genocide a name: the Holocaust.

After their victory in Germany, the Allies brought surviving leaders of the Nazi party into custody. On November 20, 1945, a trial of twenty-two Nazi party leaders began in the city of Nuremberg. In the testimony and affidavits of the prisoners and many witnesses, the name of Adolf Eichmann appeared frequently. The most damaging testimony came from Eichmann's aide Dieter Wisliceny.

Wisliceny described an important meeting with Eichmann in the summer of 1942. At the request of the Slovakian prime minister, Wisliceny had asked Eichmann to allow representatives of the Slovak government to visit Jews that had been shipped to Poland. Eichmann gave a reply that would make him the most important Nazi war criminal still at large:

> After a lengthy discussion [Wisliceny testified] Eichmann told me that this request to visit the Polish ghettos could not be granted under any circumstances whatsoever. In reply to my question, "Why?" he said that most of these Jews were no longer alive. I asked him who had given such instructions and he referred me to an order of Himmler.
>
> . . . He took a small volume of documents from his safe, turned over the pages, and showed me a letter from Himmler to the Chief of the Security Police and the SD

. . . The Fuehrer [Hitler] had ordered the final solution of the Jewish question . . . Eichmann went on to explain what was meant by this. He said that the planned biological annihilation of the Jewish race in the Eastern territories was disguised by the concept and wording "final solution."

. . . It was perfectly clear to me that this order spelled death to millions of people. I said to Eichmann, "God grant that our enemies never have the opportunity of doing the same to the German people," in reply to which Eichmann told me not to be so sentimental; it was an order of the Fuehrer's and would have to be carried out.[3]

Wisliceny appeared to the Nuremberg prosecutors as a reliable and truthful witness. His words brought Adolf Eichmann's name to the top of the list of Nazis wanted for war crimes. The Nuremberg trial ended with execution or imprisonment of eighteen prisoners and three acquittals (Wisliceny himself would be tried and executed in Bratislava, Slovakia, in 1946). But it also left several important questions unanswered. What, precisely, had Eichmann done to help the Nazis murder millions of civilians? And where was he?

Refugee From Justice

While a prisoner of the American army, Adolf Eichmann heard about the war crimes trials and of Dieter Wisliceny's testimony at Nuremberg. He realized that, sooner or later, his identity would be discovered. If the Allies found him, they would certainly put him on trial and probably put him to death.[4]

Eichmann prepared false identity papers for himself, under the name of Otto Heninger. In January 1946, while on a work detail outside of the camp, he escaped to the town of Prien on the Chemsee. He then made his way on foot to Eversen in the

Lunebürger Heide. In this remote forest of western Germany, he lived as quietly as possible, working as a lumberman and raising chickens. In the spring of 1946, he moved into a workers' barracks in the Kohlenbach forest. With about twenty other former Nazi soldiers, he worked for a private company, Bermann and Company, as a timber cutter.

On her own, Vera Liebl tried to have her husband declared legally dead. She presented an affidavit (sworn statement) by Karl Lukas, of Prague, who stated that he had witnessed Eichmann's death on April 30, 1945, in Prague. By doing this, Liebl was trying to stop the hunt for her husband. But the determined Simon Wiesenthal thwarted her by producing witnesses who had seen Eichmann alive in June 1945 in Altaussee. Wiesenthal also told the authorities that Karl Lukas was Vera Liebl's brother-in-law. The police denied Liebl's attempt to have her husband declared dead, and the hunt for Adolf Eichmann continued.

In 1948, Bermann and Company went bankrupt. Eichmann moved to Altensalzkoth, near the town of Celle, where he laid low and raised chickens. He had no intention of remaining in Germany under a false name, however. He had heard that many Nazi refugees were finding a safe harbor in Argentina, where President Juan Peron had expressed a strong sympathy for Adolf Hitler and Nazi Germany. Eichmann began saving money for the trip to South America. For him and many other Nazi leaders, Argentina was the best hope to survive the victory of the Allies.

In the Middle East, refugees of a different sort were arriving in Palestine. Jews from all over Europe, many of them concentration camp survivors, were seeking a new life far from the horrors of wartime Europe. The emigration to Palestine, however, created a bitter religious conflict. Jewish militias were fighting Muslim Arabs as well as the British, who still held governing authority in Palestine. On May 14, 1948, Israel won its independence; the new country then survived an invasion by neighboring Arab countries. For millions of Jews, Israel represented a permanent haven from the anti-Semitism that had resulted in forced emigration, deportations, and mass murder.

Escape From Europe

Eichmann remained in Altensalzkoth until the spring of 1950, when he fled Germany for Rome, the capital of Italy. He found help from an underground network of former Nazis known generally as Odessa (for Organisation der Ehemaligen SS Angehörigen, or "Organization of Former SS Members.") This group helped him with identity papers and safe houses.

Eichmann also took refuge in Catholic monasteries in Italy. The head of the German church in Italy, Bishop Alois Hudal, had supported the Nazi cause during the war. Hudal now assisted Eichmann and many other Nazi refugees to escape Europe by hiding them, providing them with visas and passports, and arranging work permits and new identity papers for them once they reached South America.

In Genoa, a northern Italian port, Eichmann obtained an entry visa from the government of Argentina. The visa allowed him to emigrate to South America. Eichmann boarded a passenger liner, the *Giovanna C*, in June 1950. The ship arrived in Buenos Aires on July 14, 1950. In October 1950, the Argentine government issued Eichmann a cedula, or official identity card, under the name of Ricardo Klement.

As Ricardo Klement, Eichmann lived in Buenos Aires, taking odd jobs to support himself until finding a responsible position with an engineering firm, CAPRI (Compania Argentina para Proyectos y Realisaciones Industrials, or

Company for Industrial Planning and Realisation). This firm was owned by Horst Carlos Fuldner, a former SS captain and a close friend of President Peron. Fuldner also owned a bank and was helping many other Germans survive in Argentina. On Fuldner's direction, CAPRI hired "Ricardo Klement" in 1952 to work in Tucuman province, northwest of Buenos Aires. Eichmann moved to the village of La Cocha in the Andes Mountains. In September 1952, he moved to Rio Portrero, where he lived with several other CAPRI workers. Eichmann helped survey water resources and land in preparation for a hydroelectric project.

In the meantime, Eichmann made contact with his wife. Around Christmas 1950, just five months after arriving in Argentina, he sent a letter home to Vera Liebl. Vera was now going by her maiden name and raising Adolf Eichmann's three sons alone. She had nearly given her husband up for dead, but after receiving the message from Argentina, Vera began planning to move her family to Argentina. She applied for a passport under the name of Veronika Liebl. There was no problem with the authorities, who did not realize at this time that Veronika Liebl was the wife of a wanted Nazi war criminal. In the spring of 1952, with their newly issued documents, the Eichmann family left Austria. Vera had booked passage on the steamer *Salta*, which arrived in Buenos Aires on July 28, 1952.

Adolf Eichmann met his family in Buenos Aires. It had been more than seven years since he had seen his wife and children. Vera introduced her sons to a man she told them was their uncle. She and her husband had decided to keep the truth hidden, to allow their children to adapt first to their new surroundings and to avoid any loose talk by the boys that might reveal who Ricardo Klement really was. A few weeks later, when he felt the time was right, Eichmann would reveal his true identity to his sons. He would talk little about his past or about his career as an SS officer. The sons of Adolf Eichmann would believe, even after his capture in 1960, that their father was an honorable and dutiful officer of the German military who, like millions of other men, had served his country and his government faithfully during the war.

Return to Buenos Aires

Soon after his family arrived in Argentina, Eichmann brought them to Rio Portrero. The family settled down in a modest house and kept to itself. The sons of Adolf Eichmann began to study Spanish with their father; when they were old enough, they went to work. Eichmann laid down some strict rules for his sons, telling them above all never to talk about him and never mention the name of Eichmann to friends or strangers.

The postwar economic boom, which had lifted the economy of Argentina, gradually slowed in the early 1950s. Many private and public companies struggled to stay afloat. CAPRI, the employer of Adolf Eichmann, did not succeed. The company went bankrupt, and Adolf Eichmann found himself without a job.

In July 1953, the Eichmanns returned to Buenos Aires, moving into a house on Chacabuco Street in the suburb of Olivos. To earn money, Eichmann opened a laundry and then a textile store. He had always been a good follower, a good soldier, and a good worker. He was polite, diligent, and very meticulous about carrying out orders, but he could not run a business by himself. One by one, his enterprises failed while his family grew larger with the birth, in the fall of 1953, of Ricardo, Adolf Eichmann's fourth son.

Simon Wiesenthal

The hunt for Adolf Eichmann after the defeat of Germany began with Simon Wiesenthal. Born in 1908 in the Ukraine, Wiesenthal later lived and worked in Lvov, in what was then eastern Poland. When the Soviet army occupied this region in 1939, Wiesenthal lost his business. In 1941, when Nazi Germany invaded, he and his wife were arrested and placed in a concentration camp. They were separated but both survived, among the few Jews to escape execution inside Poland. At the end of the war, Wiesenthal was force-marched by an SS unit to Austria, believing his wife to be long dead.

After the war's end, Wiesenthal was reunited with his wife and dedicated himself to tracking down Nazi war criminals. He worked with the U.S. Army until 1947, when he opened the Jewish Historical Documentation Center in Linz, Austria. In 1954, as interest waned in Nazi war crimes, Wiesenthal closed his office and sent all of his files to Israel—except for that of Adolf Eichmann. In the year before, he had heard that Eichmann was in Argentina, and he was determined to see him captured. The success of this mission inspired Wiesenthal to reopen the Jewish Historical Documentation Center. The center continued its work, tracking down hundreds of former Nazis over the years and seeing them captured and brought to justice.

In the meantime, Simon Wiesenthal had learned of Eichmann's presence in Buenos Aires after visiting a friend in Austria. The friend had received a letter from an acquaintance who was living in Argentina, who had the following to report: "I saw that dirty pig Eichmann who had pushed around the Jews. He lives near Buenos Aires and works for a water company."[5]

Wiesenthal passed this information to Arie Eschel, the Israeli consul in Vienna. Sure that the authorities would join the hunt, Wiesenthal felt determined to find Adolf Eichmann and bring him to justice, either in Europe or in Israel. Isser Harel, the Israeli who would lead the hunt for Eichmann several years later, said, " . . . in everything pertaining to the Jews he was the paramount authority and his were the hands that pulled the strings controlling manhunt and massacre . . . at all the Nuremberg trials of Nazi war criminals this man was pointed to as the head butcher."[6]

In fact, Simon Wiesenthal would be disappointed in his quest for several years. Many of the world's leaders, even those in the new state of Israel, were trying to forget about the war. Many believed that the most important Nazi leaders had already been captured. The trail for Adolf Eichmann would go cold, while the Eichmann family led a quiet, safe, and anonymous life in the suburbs of Buenos Aires.

The Search for Eichmann

Adolf Eichmann was now Ricardo Klement. According to his identity papers, his birthplace was Bolzano, Italy, and he had been a citizen of Germany. He kept to himself, revealing his true identity to nobody. He avoided other Nazis hiding in South America and transformed himself, to all appearances, into a dull and ordinary family man.

In the meantime, the government of Israel was making little effort to capture Nazi war criminals. Although Israeli agents worked in many foreign countries, the Israeli secret services concentrated on Arab countries and the Arab community within Israel. After the Israeli war of independence, the Israeli government saw its Arab enemies as a greater threat than the defeated Nazis. The Mossad, the Israeli foreign spy agency, and the Shin Bet, the internal intelligence organization, worked to identify and capture Arab fighters and Arab leaders. Isser Harel, the leader of the Shin Bet, also put his operatives to work in the search for

Communists and Russian agents working out of the Soviet embassy in Israel.

The Man in Olivos

For the Israeli secret services, Adolf Eichmann was a figure of history. Most believed him to still be alive, but no one knew his whereabouts. Many suspected that, like many other Nazi fugitives, he was living somewhere in South America, where nations such as Argentina were providing a safe haven for Germans who had escaped Europe after the war. The Israeli government would not spend the time, money, and manpower needed to track down Eichmann, who, if necessary, could always ask for the help of other German fugitives as well as the government of Argentina.

In September 1957, however, the Israelis received information on Eichmann that they could not ignore. A message arrived from Fritz Bauer, the attorney general for the German state of Hesse. Bauer was a Jewish lawyer, whom the Nazis had put in a concentration camp in 1933. After his release in 1936, he had escaped from Germany. After the war, he returned and made it his personal mission to seek out Nazi war criminals—often in the face of indifference or hostility on the part of German citizens.

Now Bauer had received word that a man suspected of being Adolf Eichmann was living on Chacabuco Street in Olivos. In Germany, most people were trying to forget the past. For this reason, Bauer thought it better to give the information to the Israelis. He passed the information to Walter Eytan, at the Foreign Ministry of Israel. Eytan then informed the prime minister, David Ben-Gurion. The prime minister approved an operation of the Israeli intelligence services to capture Eichmann and return him to Israel for trial.

Isser Harel knew the operation would demand careful advance planning and the most reliable possible information. Nazi war criminals in Argentina could turn for help to a large network of German refugees who protected each other in case of any emergency. If Bauer's information turned out to be incorrect, or only partially correct, Eichmann might discover the manhunt and take the opportunity to slip away. For this reason, Harel began by sending a single agent to Buenos Aires to the street address that Bauer had provided to find out if Eichmann had really been found. The agent left in January 1958 and returned in two weeks, reporting that the Olivos neighborhood was much too poor to be the residence of such an important war criminal. Harel, on hearing the report, dropped the matter.

When he learned about this, Bauer angrily demanded that Israel do more. The Israelis then asked for the name of the individual who had identified Adolf Eichmann in Olivos. At first reluctant, Bauer eventually revealed his source: Lothar Hermann, another German refugee and a resident of Olivos. Harel then sent Efraim Hofstetter, a chief of investigation for the Israeli police, to Buenos Aires to interview Hermann.

In Argentina, Hofstetter visited the Hermann family, which had moved from Olivos to the town of Coronel Suarez. Hofstetter learned that Lothar Hermann's daughter Sylvia had made friends with a young man named Klaus. This man often made anti-Semitic comments and, at one point, revealed

Jurgen Stroop (second from left, in foreground) was one of the many Nazis brought to trial and executed after the war. In this picture, he leads the attack on the Warsaw ghetto.

his true last name—Eichmann. Although Klaus had refused to give his address, Sylvia learned it from a friend. One day, out of simple curiosity, she came to the house to visit. There she encountered a middle-aged man who acted quite strangely when she mentioned that he must be the father of Klaus Eichmann.

When the Hermanns read of the war crimes trials going on in Europe and found the name Eichmann in newspaper accounts of these trials, they suspected that they had stumbled on the very same Eichmann. A much-wanted German war criminal was living in their neighborhood, and they were receiving one of his sons as a guest in their own house. Unknown to his daughter's friend, however, Lothar Hermann was Jewish and had lost both parents in the Holocaust. Hermann decided to relay his suspicions to Fritz Bauer, another name he learned from the newspaper.

Isser Harel was still not convinced. He asked Hermann to prove his statements with some hard evidence. Hermann, who was blind and who now lived with his family more than 250 miles from Olivos, only turned up the information that Eichmann was still living in Olivos under the name of Francisco Schmidt. When Mossad agents in Argentina learned that "Schmidt" was the owner of the house in Olivos—and did not live there—Harel again lost confidence in his source.

Bauer would still not give up. He flew to Israel to personally confront the Israeli authorities and challenge them to find and capture Eichmann. He revealed that a source independent of Hermann had revealed that Eichmann had left Europe under the name of Klement. Through his daughter Sylvia, Lothar Hermann had also discovered that two different names were written on the electric meter at the house in Olivos: Schmidt and Klement.

Bauer demanded a meeting in Jerusalem with Isser Harel and Chaim Cohen, the attorney general of Israel. At this meeting, Bauer insisted once again that the Israelis try to apprehend the man he suspected of being Adolf Eichmann in Argentina. Harel agreed to send Zvi Aharoni, a member of the Shin Bet, to Buenos Aries. Aharoni's only assignment was to get close to the house on Chacabuco Street and discover whether the man living there was really Adolf Eichmann.

"Mr. Klement" Moves

In the meantime, Eichmann continued to experience disappointment. He had failed running several small businesses, including a rabbit farm. Nevertheless, he bought some poor land in the distant suburbs of Buenos Aires and began building a house of his own. He had his wife buy the construction materials under her married name of Eichmann.

Eichmann's new house looked like a concrete bunker. The walls were thick, and there were no windows. Surrounding the house was a bare, treeless yard. In the meantime, he landed a job as a welder at a Mercedes-Benz automobile factory in Gonzalez Catan, about twenty miles from his new home.

In his spare time, Eichmann worked on his memoirs. He found that putting his thoughts and experiences down on paper helped him relieve the burden of living as an anonymous, invisible man who had a great deal to hide. In these memoirs, he also managed to clear himself of any guilt in the murder of millions of Jews during World War II: "I was nothing but a loyal, methodical, correct, and diligent member of the SS . . . I was neither a murderer nor a mass murderer . . . I was always a good German, I am today a good German, and I shall always be a good German!"[1]

Using a false identity, Zvi Aharoni arrived in Argentina on March 1, 1960. He came with a complete file on Eichmann, which Bauer had allowed to be copied from the files of his attorney general's office in Frankfurt, Germany. Aharoni had Eichmann's photographs, measurements, a record of his career in the SS, and a list of companies that were believed to have employed Eichmann in Argentina.

Using volunteers from Argentina's Jewish community, who were told nothing of the reasons for their missions, Aharoni discovered that the house on Chacabuco Street was now empty and that the tenants had moved. Two days after his arrival was March 3—as Aharoni knew, the birthday of Klaus Eichmann. On that day, Aharoni sent one of his volunteers to Chacabuco Street with a package and birthday greetings for "Nikolas (Klaus) Klement." The volunteer's assignment was to take the package to Chacabuco Street and learn the Klements' new address.

Workers at the house directed the volunteer to an automobile repair shop, where a son of the family worked. This young Eichmann accepted the package but would not give the new location of his family. The volunteer gave the package to the man, who was addressed as "Tito" or "Dito" by his companions. When Aharoni heard this information, he concluded that his volunteer had spoken directly with Adolf Eichmann's son Dieter, born in 1942.

Aharoni then sent a man directly to the Chacabuco Street address to ask workmen inside the house the whereabouts of "Mr. Klement." The workmen answered the questions by stating that "Klement" had moved to another suburb, a desolate patch of land known as San Fernando. For several days, Aharoni sent teams to follow Dieter home from his place of work, but each time, the volunteers lost the trail.

These identity papers were issued to Adolf Eichmann under the name "Ricardo Klement" in Tucuman, Argentina, after Eichmann had escaped from Germany.

On Monday, March 11, another one of Aharoni's young volunteers appeared at Dieter Eichmann's place of work and, by posing as a delivery boy, managed to get directions to Garibaldi Street—the location of Eichmann's house, according to one of Dieter's coworkers. Aharoni's group spent two months scouting from the bed of a truck, which was parked near the house. Hidden by a canvas tarpaulin, the volunteers watched the comings and goings and took hundreds of photographs. Aharoni's volunteers even approached Eichmann himself as land buyers, taking several pictures of him with a camera hidden inside a briefcase.

Investigating dusty public records in a local ministry, another volunteer discovered that the house in San Fernando was registered in the name of Veronica Catarina Liebl de Fichmann. On the registration, Vera Eichmann had deliberately misspelled her real last name by only one letter, so it was not well-disguised. Aharoni concluded that, without much doubt, he had Adolf Eichmann in his sights—and that his prey had done a rather sloppy job of evading pursuit.

Closing In

On March 21, the observation team got the final proof they sought. On that day, they observed the man they believed to be Eichmann returning to his house with a bouquet of flowers. They heard a celebration taking place inside the house and observed the children dressed up as if for a party. They knew, from Eichmann's file, that March 21 was the date of his marriage, twenty-five years previously, to Vera Liebl.

The Israeli secret service decided to kidnap the man they suspected was Adolf Eichmann, get him to confess who he really was, then bring him back to Israel for a trial. For this operation they would need thorough preparation, good luck, and a little cooperation from their intended target.

To carry out the mission, a ten-person team gathered in Buenos Aires under the overall command of Isser Harel. Rafi Eitan, the chief of operations of the Shin Bet, would direct the operation by posing as a British businessman. Aharoni also posed as a businessman, while a doctor, whose mission was to sedate Eichmann if necessary, and a document expert, who could prepare false passports and driver's licenses, also joined the team. Also on the team were Zvi Malchin, a Polish Jew and a weapons and explosives expert, and Zeev Keren, a carpenter whose job it was to build a secret room for holding Eichmann while the team prepared to get him out of the country.

The team moved into safe houses in and near Buenos Aires, rented two large cars, and laid their plans. They were breaking the laws of Argentina, of course, and they had to work in secret. They knew that Argentina and other South American nations had already provided safe haven for many fleeing Nazis. They also knew that Eichmann belonged to a network of German refugees who provided safe haven and an escape, if necessary, when one of their members faced extradition (being forced out of the country). The Israeli team could not count on any help in their task or protection if they should be discovered and arrested. They were operating alone.

With binoculars and a notebook, members of the team kept a constant watch on Eichmann's house from a nearby railway embankment. On May 11, at about 7:25 in the evening, the team drove their two cars to Garibaldi Street and waited for Eichmann's bus to appear. In the lead car were Aharoni, Malchin, Eitan, and Zeev Keren. This car was parked on the right side of the street leading to the house. The second car was parked near the corner. Its three passengers, including the doctor, were to observe and lend help if anything should go wrong. The driver of the second car also had a very simple task: to turn on his lights as soon as Eichmann got off the bus. Shining toward the corner and away from the kidnap scene, the lights would make it harder for him and any other passersby to see the kidnap car.

It helped the kidnap team that Eichmann kept to a strict daily routine. Each day, at about 7:40 in the evening, he alighted from a bus and walked a few hundred yards to his home. At that time, the sun was setting, and the streets were growing dark. Eichmann always walked alone, and it would be difficult for any bystander from the main road to see anything happening on Garibaldi Street. There seemed no better place for the operation than Eichmann's own neighborhood.

On the evening of May 11, however, and much to the surprise of the Israeli agents, Eichmann broke his usual regular schedule. When the 7:40 bus made its regular stop, he did not appear. The team waited, prepared to leave if too much time should go by and their presence begin to attract notice. Just after 8:00 P.M., another bus appeared. Adolf Eichmann climbed down and walked his normal route toward home.

Malchin turned from his position at the driver's side door and confronted Eichmann. He spoke the only word of Spanish he had learned: "momentito!" Eichmann stopped. Malchin grabbed him, and the two men went tumbling into the ditch by the side of the road. Keren and Eitan jumped out of the back of the car, while Eichmann kicked and screamed. Finally, after several minutes, Eichmann was wrestled into the backseat of the car, which sped off. After getting well clear of the neighborhood, Keren switched the car's regular plates to diplomatic plates. Although the team made sure not to break any traffic laws, the diplomatic plates made it even less likely that the police would stop their car.

The team brought Eichmann to the safe house, placed him on a bed, and handcuffed him to a bedpost. Aharoni interrogated the prisoner. Eichmann admitted who he was, gave all the names he had used in the past, and also admitted that he belonged to the SS and the Nazi party. But when Aharoni told him that he would be brought to Israel to stand trial, Eichmann resisted. He would agree to a trial but said it must be held in Germany or Argentina. Aharoni refused, pointing out that these two countries would have no interest in holding such a trial. He promised Eichmann a fair trial and told him that he could choose his own defense lawyer.

Eichmann then wrote and signed a statement, in which he agreed to go to Israel to face a trial: "I, the undersigned, Adolf Eichmann, state herewith of my own free will, since my true identity has been revealed, that there is no point in my continuing to evade justice. I declare myself willing to proceed to Israel and to stand trial there before a competent court."[2]

Eichmann's statement gave the Israelis the legal cover they needed once their prisoner was in Israel. If Eichmann changed his mind, claimed not to be who he really was, or claimed to have been forced against his will to stand trial in Israel, this signed statement would prove otherwise.

A Secret Plane Trip

Eichmann's disappearance immediately alarmed his wife and his sons. Veronika Eichmann went to the police and claimed that robbers had kidnapped her husband. She did not, of course, reveal her husband's true identity—to the police and the government, Adolf Eichmann was Ricardo Klement, an ordinary, working-class German immigrant.

In the meantime, Eichmann's son Klaus went to the Mercedes-Benz factory where Eichmann had been working, revealed his father's identity as a former SS officer to several of Eichmann's coworkers, and asked for help. Klaus also went to the police—this time, claiming that Ricardo Klement was not his father but his uncle. The conflicting stories about Adolf Eichmann prevented the Argentine police from ever suspecting the truth or solving the kidnapping until Israel announced Eichmann's capture to the world.

The Israeli team had one difficult task to complete: smuggling their prisoner out of Argentina. They knew that May 19, 1960, was the 150th anniversary of the independence of Argentina and that leaders from all over the world would arrive to take part in the festivities. On May 18, Israel sent its own representatives, including cabinet ministers and military officers, aboard the first flight of its national airline, El Al, from Israel to Argentina.

Two days later, in the early evening of May 20, the crew of the El Al plane prepared for takeoff and the return flight to Israel. While the pilot went through a takeoff checklist, a crew on the ground refueled the plane. After midnight, in the early morning hours of May 21, several cars approached the plane, stopping near the stairway ramp parked at the plane's cabin doors. The Israeli kidnap team had brought Adolf Eichmann to the Buenos Aires airport, drugged him to make him sleepy and cooperative, and then marched him up the stairway to the waiting plane. As soon as Eichmann was on the plane, the pilot took off. Customs guards at the airport paid no attention. The engineer of the Holocaust, one of the world's most wanted Nazi war criminals, was now in the custody of the Israeli government.

8

The Trial of Adolf Eichmann

On May 23, 1960, Prime Minister David Ben-Gurion rose before the Knesset, the legislature of Israel, to make an important announcement. The gathered lawmakers, who were preparing for a routine day of business, sat in stunned silence as Ben-Gurion's words rang through the hall:

> I have to inform the Knesset that a short time ago one of the greatest Nazi war criminals, Adolf Eichmann, who together with other Nazi leaders collaborated in the so-called Final Solution of the Jewish question— namely, the extermination of six million European Jews—was found by the Israeli Secret Services.[1]

While Ben-Gurion was speaking to the Knesset, Israel was making careful preparations for Eichmann. An entire prison complex near Jerusalem was cleared of its regular prisoners. A team of border police was assigned to guard Eichmann. To prevent any acts of revenge against Eichmann, the government conducted background checks on each guard. Israel did not permit anybody who had been in a concentration camp or who had lost relatives to the Nazis to serve. Nor did they allow anyone who spoke German or Yiddish, a Jewish dialect similar to German, to guard Eichmann. Surveillance teams kept an eye on the prison and its surroundings at all times.

Within the prison, Eichmann lived in a ten-by-thirteen-foot cell, where he was provided with a cot, a table, and a chair. A guard was present inside the cell at all times, day and night; a single bare electric lightbulb shone at all hours. A second guard was posted in the room immediately outside the cell, while a third guard stood watch in the corridor. The guards were there to make sure Eichmann did not follow the example of Hitler and Heinrich Himmler by taking his own life and thus escaping justice altogether.

Interrogation

A special team of Israeli police officers known as Bureau 06 was assigned the task of interrogating Eichmann before the trial. To prepare, the members of the team studied books about the Holocaust and about the war crimes trials. One of the Nuremberg prosecutors, an American lawyer named Robert Kempner, came to Israel to offer his advice and knowledge. Bureau 06 also requested documents from countries throughout Europe to back up the case against Adolf Eichmann for war crimes. Every country cooperated—with the exception of the Soviet Union, which considered the events of World War II in Soviet territory to be a state secret.

During this time, Adolf Eichmann spent thirty-five days with Captain Avner W. Less, his Israeli interrogator. Less recorded his questions and Eichmann's responses on reel-to-reel tape. The transcript of questions and answers ran to 3,564 pages.[2] Eichmann took this opportunity to give a complete description of his life and his version of everything he had done as a member of the Nazi party.

At every turn, Eichmann explained his actions as that of a man who simply followed orders and who had no choice in the matter. In the final hours of the long interrogation, he took the opportunity to state: "All my life I have been accustomed to obedience, from early childhood to May 8, 1945—an obedience which in my years of membership in the SS became blind and unconditional. What would I have gained by disobedience? And whom would it have served?"[3]

The Charges

In the meantime, the Israeli prosecutors prepared their case against Adolf Eichmann. They gathered documents—letters, official reports, orders, the minutes of meetings—captured in the last months of the war by the Allies in Germany. They collected statements from witnesses in Israel and Europe, as well as testimony from other war crimes trials. Most importantly, they used the confessions and explanations Eichmann made to Captain Less.

Using this material and the interrogations conducted by Captain Less, the Israeli attorney general, Gideon Hausner, prepared a fifteen-count indictment: four counts of crimes against the Jewish people, eight counts of crimes against humanity, and three counts of membership in criminal organizations, including the SS, the SD, and the Gestapo. If convicted on any of the first twelve counts, Eichmann could be put to death, while a conviction of "membership in criminal organizations" carried a prison sentence.

Israel also offered Eichmann a choice of a defense lawyer to represent him. One of these candidates, Dr. Robert Servatius, had called on Eichmann's relations in Linz and had offered his services. Servatius, a former German army officer, had already served as a defense counsel at Nuremberg. With the recommendation of his brother-in-law, who was also a lawyer, Eichmann selected Servatius as his defense lawyer.

Many countries protested the capture of Adolf Eichmann and his trial in Israel. According to normal legal procedure, Nazi leaders had always been tried where they had committed their crimes, particularly Germany, Austria, and Italy. To try Eichmann in Israel, to have his prosecution organized by Jewish lawyers and his verdict and sentence pronounced by Jewish Israeli judges, seemed to many a denial of his right to a just and fair trial.

The loudest such protest came from the government of Argentina. The kidnapping and deportation of Eichmann violated that country's laws. In some cases, the Argentine government had refused Israeli requests to extradite former Nazis, including Dr. Josef Mengele, the infamous "angel of death." At the gates of Auschwitz, Mengele had selected prisoners to be sent immediately to the gas chambers. He had also carried out gruesome medical experiments on the camp's prisoners. These crimes, in the eyes of the Argentine government, did not merit his extradition to Israel for trial.

But in August 1960, Argentina and Israel settled their differences over the kidnapping of Adolf Eichmann, issuing a joint declaration to this effect. (Eventually, after the Eichmann affair, Argentina also agreed to extradite Josef Mengele—by which time Mengele had escaped to neighboring Paraguay.) According to the laws of Argentina, Eichmann had sacrificed

---

Dr. Josef Mengele was never brought to justice. He was reported to have drowned in 1979. In 1985, his remains were found. Tests proved that they were indeed his.

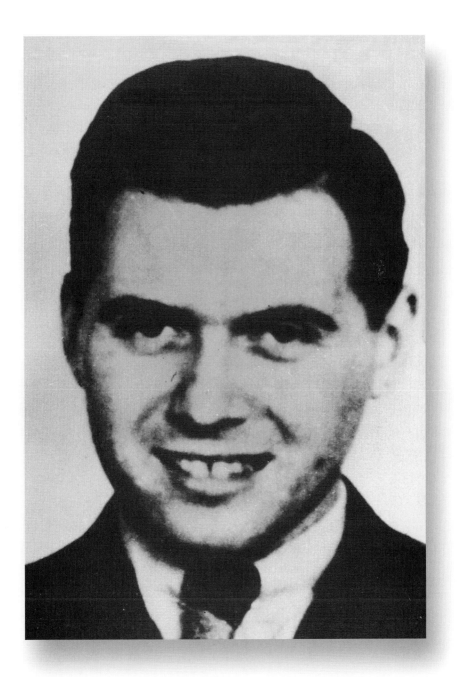

his right for asylum and protection by declaring his German nationality and a false name on his new identity papers. Although kidnapping was certainly a crime, Eichmann could not claim the same rights as an ordinary citizen of that country. Nor did he ask for asylum from West Germany. In fact, Eichmann had not resisted his capture; he had admitted his true identity of his own free will, and he had come to Israel prepared to stand trial.

In Linz, Austria, Eichmann's brothers Otto and Robert protested the kidnapping and trial. Robert denied that Israel's captive was Adolf Eichmann, while Otto wrote the following of his brother in a letter to a German magazine: "He was a tolerant and sympathetic man. He was not politically minded. Everybody liked him and he joined the SS because of his military fervor. . . . There are documents which show that my brother helped many Jews because of his wonderful heart."[4]

Although many people knew Eichmann to be responsible for war crimes, they still doubted that Israel could give Eichmann a fair trial. Eichmann's own defense counsel, Dr. Robert Servatius, made this point at the beginning of the trial. The judge presiding responded: "It cannot be denied that the memory of the Nazi holocaust stirs every Jew, but while this case is being tried before us it will be our duty to restrain these feelings, and this duty we shall honor."[5]

Prime Minister David Ben-Gurion would not change his mind about putting Adolf Eichmann on trial. Determined to put the crimes of Nazi Germany before the world, Ben-Gurion also believed the trial would educate the younger generation that had not experienced the horrors of World War II. To achieve this goal, Ben-Gurion allowed television cameras into the District Court of Jerusalem, making the Eichmann trial the first, in the history of television, to be broadcast.

A Trial Before the World

The trial of Adolf Eichmann began on April 11, 1961, with three Israeli judges presiding. Carpenters built a bulletproof glass booth for the defendant to protect him from any assassination attempt. Eichmann sat between two armed guards and listened to a German translation of the Hebrew proceedings over a pair of earphones. The three judges sat on a raised bench in front of the court, while tables for the defense and prosecution teams faced the judges.

In the eyes of the judges and of the government of Israel, the court represented not the Jews of any particular place or country, but all Jews everywhere who had suffered in common at the hands of Eichmann and the Nazis. As the only country that represented the Jews of the world, the judges believed Israel had the right to try Eichmann for the crimes he had committed against the Jews of Europe.

The prosecution had taken hundreds of applications from Israeli citizens eager to testify about their experience of the Holocaust. The prosecution team selected one hundred witnesses, ninety of whom had survived imprisonment at the hands of the Nazis. The testimony of these prosecution witnesses began on April 24 and lasted for 121 court sessions.[6] At the same time, the prosecution introduced documents from Eichmann's fellow officers, staff members, and others who had firsthand knowledge of his actions during the war.

Most of the prosecution witnesses had never met Adolf Eichmann in person or had any knowledge of exactly what he had done. Instead, they testified to the Holocaust itself, describing how it was to live in Auschwitz, Treblinka, Chelmno, and other death camps. They described the actions of the Einsatzgruppen and the life of the urban prisons known as ghettos. The first witness, Zindel Grynszpan, was the

father of Herschel Grynszpan, whose assassination of Ernst vom Rath in Paris had touched off the Kristallnacht, the night of riot and murder against German Jews that had taken place in November 1938. It was Zindel Grynszpan's arrest by the German police and his deportation to Poland that had inspired Herschel Grynszpan to murder Vom Rath.

Before a hushed court in Jerusalem, Grynszpan told the story of how he was taken from his home and, with about twelve thousand other Jews that had been rounded up as well, brought to Poland: "The S.S. men were whipping us, those who lingered they hit, and blood was flowing on the road. . . . They shouted at us, 'Run! Run!' I was hit and fell into the ditch. My son helped me, and he said: 'Run, Father, run, or you'll die!'"[7]

The writings of those personally acquainted with Adolf Eichmann provided the most powerful evidence against him. During session 16, the prosecution submitted a report of Dieter Wisliceny, Eichmann's longtime acquaintance and, during World War II, one of his most trusted aides. Wisliceny had written the following on October 26 and November 18, 1946, while imprisoned in Bratislava, Slovakia.

> Hitler's order to get rid of all the commissars and active leaders of the Communist Party, issued at the outbreak of the war with Soviet Russia, signals a new stage in the brutalization of the War. . . . In this "Commissars' Order" Eichmann saw a possibility of exterminating the remaining Jews.

Protected by a booth of bulletproof glass, defendant Adolf Eichmann takes notes during his trial on war crimes in Jerusalem.

By agreement with Mueller and Heydrich he began, in the autumn of 1941, to expel Jews from the confines of the Reich, Austria, Bohemia and Moravia towards those areas in which the "Commissars' Order" was valid, principally to Riga and to Minsk. In Riga, Eichmann's friend Stahlecker was the head of the Einsatzgruppe. . . .

From the summer of 1941 Eichmann began in an increasing measure, to deal with the Jews of Poland. In various instances, he himself, apparently following an order by Himmler, carried out mass executions in Poland too. In particular his relations became closer with the "Chief of the SS and Police" in Lublin, the man who had been the Austrian Gauleiter, Odilo Globocnik, whom Eichmann had already known from Austria.

According to the details which Eichmann himself related to me, Globocnik was the first person who operated gas chambers for the mass extermination of human beings. In the area under his command, Globocnik set up large work camps for Jews; he got rid of those who were unfit for work in the manner described. According to Eichmann's explanations, Globocnik's "process" was "less likely to attract attention" than mass shootings, seeing that in various instances units of the police refused to carry out the execution of women and children.[8]

During the seventeenth session, the prosecution read from the memoirs of Rudolf Höss, the commandant of the Auschwitz death camp. In his memoirs, Höss describes a meeting with Heinrich Himmler, who told him of Hitler's orders for the Final Solution, the murder of the Jews. Himmler added that Adolf Eichmann would be the man responsible for organizing the rounding up and transport of Jews. Eichmann would soon come personally to Auschwitz to make the necessary arrangements with Höss.

According to the memoirs of Höss:

After a short while Eichmann came to me at Auschwitz. He confidentially revealed to me the plans which were in operation for every country. . . . First to be considered, as far as Auschwitz was concerned, were Eastern Upper Silesia and parts of the general government [central Poland] which adjoined it. Simultaneously and following on thereafter, dependent on the situation, would come the Jews from Germany and Czechoslovakia. Closely after this—the West, France, Belgium and Holland. He even mentioned to me the numbers of the anticipated transports but I am no longer able to quote them. We also spoke about carrying out the extermination. It was said that only gas could be considered since the disposal of the expected masses by shooting was simply an impossibility and it also involved too great a burden on the SS personnel who were to be entrusted with the implementation—in view of the women and children.

Eichmann gave me an explanation of extermination by means of emissions of gas from truck engines, as had been carried out until then in the East. But such a method, according to him, could not be applied to the mass transports expected at Auschwitz. . . . Eichmann wanted to find out about a gas which was easy to secure and which did not require any special installations, and advise me thereafter. We proceeded to the area in order to determine a suitable site.[9]

British troops had captured Höss in March 1946. The British had turned Höss over to the government of Poland, which tried him for war crimes. He was found guilty, sentenced to death, and hanged at the Auschwitz camp on April 16, 1947. Even though Höss was long dead and could not testify in person at the trial, his words condemned Eichmann as one of the individuals responsible for the mechanics of death camps such as Auschwitz.

Adolf Eichmann agreed to appear on the witness stand at his own trial. His testimony began on June 20 and continued for

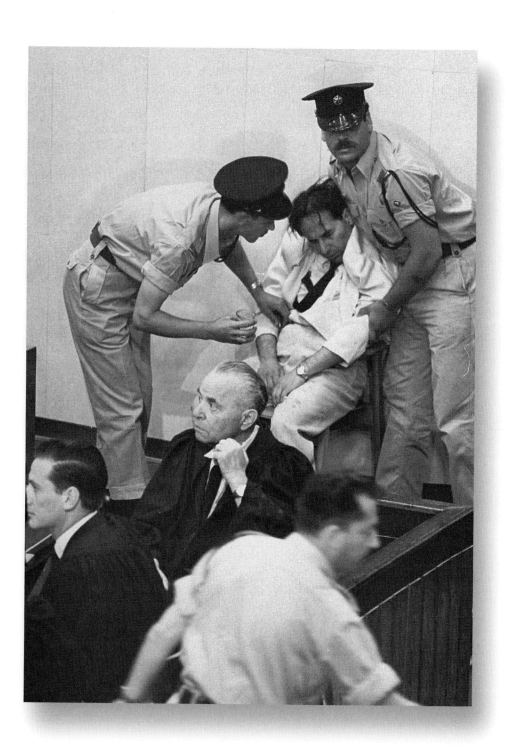

fourteen court sessions. The prosecution then cross-examined him for seventeen sessions.

Eichmann defended himself by stating that, at all times when he acted against the Jews, he had been following orders from his superiors. He had committed no violence himself or harmed a single Jew. Instead, Eichmann claimed, his long study of Zionism and the Hebrew language before the war showed that he held the Jews in high regard. He was simply one officer among many, one who carried out orders, which he had no right, as a military man, to question.

Eichmann also pointed out that the Holocaust had not been his idea. Rather, Hitler, Himmler, and Heydrich had laid the detailed plans in order to see millions of Jews murdered in the camps. Eichmann's role had only been that of a transporter, an officer responsible for getting the Jews and other captives from one place to another.

When asked about his reasons for joining the Nazi party, Eichmann replied that he had agreed with Hitler's idea of fighting against the Versailles treaty. The question of the Jews had not concerned him at all—when Hitler promised that the Jews would be annihilated in the "next war," Eichmann testified that he had believed Hitler had meant political annihilation, not murder.

Eichmann told the judges that he had believed in the complete separation of Jews from Germany—by emigration. He took great pride in the operations of the emigration office in Vienna. This office worked in his opinion, toward a goal that was satisfactory to both the Jews and the Nazi

This survivor, who testified at the Eichmann trial, was so overcome with emotion that he fainted.

Adolf Eichmann's Final Statement

After Eichmann was found guilty, the court allowed him to make a final statement before sentencing. In the excerpt below, Eichmann says that he was only following orders. He felt that the court should show mercy because of this and not give him the death penalty.

> It was my misfortune to become entangled in these atrocities. But these misdeeds did not happen according to my wishes. It was not my wish to slay people. The guilt for the mass murder is solely that of the political leaders.
>
> I did try to leave my position, to leave for the front, for honest battle. But I was held fast in those dark duties. Once again I would stress that I am guilty of having been obedient, having subordinated myself to my official duties and the obligations of war service and my oath of allegiance and my oath of office, and in addition, once the war started, there was also martial law.
>
> This obedience was not easy. And again, anyone who has to give orders and has to obey orders knows what one can demand of people. I did not persecute Jews with avidity and passion. That is what the government did. Nor could the persecution be carried out other than by a government. But I never . . . I accuse the leaders of abusing my obedience. At that time obedience was demanded, just as in the future it will also be demanded of the subordinate. Obedience is commended as a virtue.[10]

government. When, after the outbreak of the war, an entirely different kind of operation began in Poland, Eichmann testified to feeling great distress. He was repelled by the murders and cruelties carried out in the concentration camps and by the roaming Einsatzgruppen. However, he said that he could do nothing about it—he was a soldier, it was wartime, and the law of his land as set down by the Nazi government enforced strict obedience.

The trial of Adolf Eichmann closed on August 14, after 114 court sessions. The judges called a recess that lasted for four months. On December 11, the court reconvened to recite its judgement on the defendant. The judgement ran to 240 sections and took two full days to read out.[11] While the prosecution demanded the death penalty, Servatius argued for mercy, claiming that Eichmann was not personally guilty of the murder of anybody.

The court passed sentence on Adolf Eichmann on December 15, 1961: death by hanging. Eichmann would be the first person ever to be sentenced to death by an Israeli court. He appealed his sentence to the Israeli Court of Appeal, the highest court in the land. During the appeal, which began on March 22, 1962, Dr. Servatius again argued that the trial had been both illegal and unjust and that Eichmann still had the right, by international law, to be extradited and tried in Germany, where the crimes of which he was accused had actually taken place. The appeal was denied on May 29. On the same day, Eichmann sent a handwritten plea for mercy to President Itzhak Ben-Zvi, including letters from his wife and family. The plea was denied, and on May 31, Adolf Eichmann was hanged. His body was cremated and the Israeli government ordered his ashes scattered in the Mediterranean Sea, well outside the country's territorial waters.

A New Healing Begins

The terrible crimes of the Nazis had faded in the memory of people around the world, while men, women, and children tried to forget World War II and its many horrors. The arrest and trial of Adolf Eichmann reopened very painful wounds, yet it kept the world's attention through print and television for more than a year. When the case closed with Eichmann's execution on May 31, 1962, the subject of the Holocaust had been opened for discussion. Scholars, students, historians, and survivors began talking, writing, and arguing about the genocide committed by the Nazis in an attempt to know it, understand it, and prevent it from happening again.

The nations of Europe had rebuilt and moved on after the war. Germany was divided into East and West Germany, with the east subject to a Communist government backed by the Soviet Union. West Germany made its peace with France and with the many other nations Nazi Germany had subjected to conquest and occupation during the war. Many people within Germany now wanted to simply forget about the Nazis and about the crimes committed by Adolf Eichmann and others like him. They may have hoped that the hanging of Eichmann would close the book, permanently, on this ugly chapter in their history.

Eichmann's trial and execution, however, had the opposite effect, inspiring renewed interest in the Holocaust. The hunt for Nazi war criminals continued in earnest. New books appeared on the subject; new discoveries won headlines in the newspapers and attention from television broadcasters.

Adolf Eichmann stands at attention and listens as he is sentenced to death by the court.

Rudolf Kastner

A leader of Hungary's Zionist movement, Rudolf (Israel) Kastner played a key role in the "Jewish lives for trucks" offer, in which ten thousand Allied trucks were to be given to the Nazis in exchange for sparing the lives of Budapest Jews in 1944. This deal failed, but during the negotiations, Kastner did manage to help more than sixteen hundred Jews to safety in Switzerland.

After the war, Kastner left Hungary for Israel, where he served as a government minister and a leader of the Labor party. However, many Israelis believed Kastner to be a collaborator, who had actually helped the Nazis in order to save his own skin and that of his relatives and friends. Kastner was also accused of helping the Nazis by deceiving the Hungarian Jews about the true destination of trains leaving Hungary for Poland—the death camp at Auschwitz.

In 1954, the government of Israel accused another Jewish Hungarian survivor, Malkhiel Gruenvald, of slandering Kastner. At the trial, Gruenvald repeated the accusation that Kastner had been a collaborator. Gruenvald was found innocent by the court, but the judge in the trial also sharply criticized Kastner for his activities during the war.

The trial cost Kastner his reputation and, perhaps, his life. On March 4, 1957, he was assassinated in Israel by Ze'ev Ekstein, a former member of the Israeli Secret Service.

Nazi-hunters such as Simon Wiesenthal continued their efforts to find Hitler's war criminals and bring them to justice.

Historians and philosophers such as Hannah Arendt saw the Eichmann trial as an opportunity to examine the nature of totalitarian governments, which carry out genocide through an apparatus of hardworking and obedient functionaries such as Eichmann who learn to put their consciences aside while obeying the wishes of their superiors.

To many historians of Nazi Germany and the Holocaust, Adolf Eichmann became an example of the "banality of evil," a phrase coined by Arendt in her book *Eichmann in Jerusalem*. He had no special allegiance to Hitler's cause and always claimed he was not anti-Semitic. He was a bland, dull individual with intelligence but with little imagination or passion. He was unfit for leadership—a careerist whose best virtues were obedience and diligence. Yet he diligently helped to carry out murder on a massive scale, with little hesitation or self-doubt. For this reason, of all the Nazi war criminals caught and tried after the war, Eichmann may have been the most frightening. His anti-Semitism had turned him from a traveling salesman into an accessory to genocide. He was an example of the ability to work without conscience of right or wrong, to serve in a vast killing machine and still believe that he was doing good.

TIMELINE

(Shaded areas indicate events in the life of Adolf Eichmann.)

1906

Adolf Eichmann is born in Solingen, Germany, on March 19.

1913

The Eichmann family moves to Linz, Austria.

1914

World War I begins.

1918

Germany signs an armistice ending World War I.

1921

Adolf Eichmann begins studies at the Linz Higher Federal College for Electrotechnology, Engineering, and Construction.

1925

Eichmann becomes a salesman for Oberösterreichische Elektrobau.

1927

Eichmann joins the Vacuum Oil Company as a salesman in Upper Austria.

1931

Eichmann is engaged to Veronika (Vera) Liebl.

1932

Ernst Kaltenbrunner recruits Adolf Eichmann into the Nazi party.

1933

Adolf Hitler is named chancellor of Germany. The Nazi party swiftly takes control of the German government. In the same year, the Vacuum Oil Company fires Adolf Eichmann.

Hitler becomes Chancellor of Germany.

March 22: Concentration camp at Dachau opens.

April 26: Gestapo established.

May 10: Nazis burn banned books in public.

1934

August 2: Hitler names himself "Führer," or leader, of Germany.

1935

The Nuremberg Laws revoke the citizenship and suspend legal rights of Jews living within Germany. Adolf Eichmann joins Department II 112, the branch of the Sicherheitsdienst (SD) dealing with the "Jewish Question."

1936

Nazis boycott Jewish-owned businesses.

March 7: Nazis occupy Rhineland.

May 31: Jews in Germany no longer allowed to serve in armed forces.

July: Sachsenhausen concentration camp opened.

September 15: Anti-Jewish Nuremberg Laws are enacted; Jews are no longer considered citizens of Germany.

1937

Eichmann travels to the Middle East to investigate conditions and the possibility of forcing Jewish emigration to Palestine.

July 15: Buchenwald concentration camp opens.

1938

Nazi Germany annexes Austria. Adolf Eichmann becomes the head of the Vienna Office for Jewish Emigration. In November, Jews throughout Germany and Austria are assaulted and their property seized or destroyed during Kristallnacht.

Jews are attacked in Germany and Austria during Kristallnacht.

March: Mauthausen concentration camp opens.

March 13: Germany annexes Austria and applies all anti-Jewish laws there.

1938 *(continued)*

July 6: League of Nations holds conference on Jewish refugees at Evian, France, but no action is taken to help the refugees.

October 5: All Jewish passports must now be stamped with a red "J."

October 15: Nazi troops occupy the Sudentenland.

November 9-10: Kirstallnacht, the Night of the Broken Glass; Jewish businesses and synagogues are destroyed and thirty thousand Jews are sent to concentration camps.

1939

Eichmann sets up an office for Jewish Emigration in Prague, the capital of Czechoslovakia. In September, Germany invades Poland, starting World War II in Europe.

Hitler invades Poland; World War II begins; SS begins killing Polish intellectuals and Jews.

March: Germany invades Bohemia and Moravia.

March 15: Germans occupy Czechoslovakia.

August 23: Germany and the Soviet Union sign a non-aggression pact.

September 1: Germany invades Poland, beginning World War II.

October 28: First Polish ghetto established in Piotrkow.

November 23: Jews in Poland are forced to wear an arm band or yellow star.

1940

The Germans build forced-labor camps in occupied Poland. Under Eichmann's orders, Section IV B 4 of the Gestapo begins transporting Jews to labor camps and urban ghettos.

Polish Jews are moved into ghettos in major cities.

April 9: Germans occupy Denmark and southern Norway.

1940 *(continued)*

May 7: Lodz Ghetto is established.

May 20: Auschwitz concentration camp is established.

June 22: France surrenders to Germany.

September 27: Germany, Italy and Japan form the Axis powers.

November 16: Warsaw Ghetto is established.

1941

Germany invades Russia; SS begins rounding up Jews inside Russian territory.

June 22: Germany invades the Soviet Union.

October: Auschwitz II (Birkenau) death camp is established.

1942

Eichmann assists in setting up a system of mass execution in the labor camps of Poland.

January 20: Wannsee Conference in Berlin where the "Final Solution" is outlined.

March 17: Killings begin at Belzec death camp.

May: Killings begin at Sobibor death camp.

July 22: Treblinka concentration camp is established.

Summer-Winter: Mass deportations to death camps begin.

1943

Eichmann arrives in Slovakia to persuade the Slovakian government to deport Jews to Poland. He also oversees deportations from France, the Low Countries, Norway, and Bulgaria.

Nazis lose Battle of Stalingrad; war turns against Germany.

March: Liquidation of Krakow Ghetto begins.

April 19: Warsaw ghetto uprising.

Fall: Liquidation of Minsk, Vilna, and Riga ghettos.

1944

Eichmann arrives in Hungary to set up a headquarters in Budapest. He organizes mass deportations of Hungarian Jews to Poland.

March 19: Germans invade and occupy Hungary; Eichmann arrives.

May 15: Jewish deportations from Hungary begin, most sent to Auschwitz.

June 24: Budapest Jews moved to yellow-star houses.

July 14: Soviet forces liberate Majdanek death camp.

October 20: Jewish draft for labor brigades begins.

November 2: Soviets break through defenses near Budapest; Jews in labor brigades massacred by Hungarian soldiers.

November 8: Death marches to Hegyeshalom begin.

December 8: Soviet siege of Budapest begins.

December 22: Eichmann attempts to assassinate Jewish Council; leaves Budapest.

December 24: Increased terrorism against Jews begins, including raids of legation offices, protected houses, children's homes, and hospitals.

1945

Soviet and Allied armies defeat Nazi Germany.

SS abandons concentration camps to Allies; Hitler commits suicide.

Auschwitz inmates begin death march.

April 6–10: Buchenwald inmates sent on death march.

April 30: Hitler commits suicide.

May 8: Germany surrenders.

1946

In January, Eichmann goes underground after escaping an American prisoner-of-war camp. He begins working for a lumber company in a remote German forest.

1948

Eichmann's employer goes bankrupt and he loses his job. Eichmann begins to prepare for a flight to South America.

1950

Eichmann flees Germany for Italy. In June, he boards a ship and moves to Argentina. He takes out new identity papers under the name of Ricardo Klement.

1952

Eichmann moves to Tucuman, Argentina, to work for a hydroelectric company. In the fall, his wife and three sons arrive in Argentina.

1953

Eichmann moves to Olivos, a suburb of Buenos Aires. His fourth son, Ricardo, is born.

1957

Through a German attorney general, Israel learns that Adolf Eichmann is living in Argentina.

1958

The Israeli secret services send agents to Argentina to find Adolf Eichmann.

1960

A team of Israelis kidnaps Eichmann from his home and brings him back to Israel. Eichmann is interrogated and indicted for war crimes.

1961

The trial of Adolf Eichmann begins on April 11 and lasts for 114 sessions. On December 11, the court convicts Eichmann and sentences him to death.

1962

Adolf Eichmann is executed on May 31.

Chapter Notes

Introduction: Eichmann on the Run

1. From Dachau Liberated: The Official Report by the U.S. Seventh Army; quoted in *The Liberation of Dachau*, n.d., <http://www.scrapbookpages.com/DachauScrapbook/Dachau Liberation/> (January 26, 2004).

Chapter 1. Eichmann and Hitler in Austria

1. Jochen Von Lang and Claus Sibyll, eds., *Eichmann Interrogated: Transcripts from the Archives of the Israeli Police* (New York: Da Capo Press, 1999), p. 11.

2. Hannah Arendt, *Eichmann in Jerusalem: A Report on the Banality of Evil* (New York: Penguin Books, 1994), p. 33.

3. Von Lang and Sibyll, pp. 18–19.

4. Arendt, p. 39.

5. Deborah Dwork and Robert Jan van Pelt, *Holocaust: A History* (New York: Norton, 2002), p. 113.

Chapter 2. In the Service of the Nazi Party

1. Jochen Von Lang and Claus Sibyll, eds., *Eichmann Interrogated: Transcripts from the Archives of the Israeli Police* (New York: Da Capo Press, 1999), pp. 43–44.

2. Hannah Arendt, *Eichmann in Jerusalem: A Report on the Banality of Evil* (New York: Penguin Books, 1994), p. 45.

3. Michael Berenbaum in *Eichmann Interrogated: Transcripts from the Archives of the Israel Police*, eds. Jochen Von Lang and Claus Sibyll (New York: Da Capo Press, 1999), pp. x–xi.

4. Peter Z. Malkin and Harry Stein, *Eichmann in My Hands* (New York: Warner Books, 1990), p. 57.

5. Von Lang and Sibyll, p. 57.

Chapter 3. Preparing for the Final Solution

1. Deborah Dwork and Robert Jan van Pelt, *Holocaust: A History* (New York: Norton, 2002), p. 113.

2. Jochen Von Lang and Claus Sibyll, eds., *Eichmann Interrogated: Transcripts from the Archives of the Israeli Police* (New York: Da Capo Press, 1999), p. 67.

3. Ibid., p. 76.

4. Quentin Reynolds, *Minister of Death: The Adolf Eichmann Story* (New York: The Viking Press, 1960), pp. 142–143.

Chapter 4. The Final Solution Across Europe

1. John Donovan, *Eichmann: Mastermind of the Holocaust* (New York: Kensington Publishing Group, 1978), p. 193.

2. Quentin Reynolds, *Minister of Death: The Adolf Eichmann Story* (New York: The Viking Press, 1960), pp. 133–134.

3. From The Trial of Adolf Eichmann, Session 32, *The Nizkor Project*, n.d., <http://www.vex.net/~nizkor/hweb/people/e/eichmann-adolf/transcripts/Sessions/Session-032-03.html> (January 27, 2004).

4. Hannah Arendt, *Eichmann in Jerusalem: A Report on the Banality of Evil* (New York: Penguin Books, 1994), pp. 191–192.

5. Ibid., p. 171.

6. Martin Gilbert, *The Holocaust: A History of the Jews of Europe During the Second World War* (New York: Holt, Reinhart, and Winston, 1985), p. 614.

7. Israel Gutman, ed. *Encyclopedia of the Holocaust*, vol. 3, (New York: Macmillan, 1990), p. 909.

Chapter 5. Eichmann in Hungary

1. Quentin Reynolds, *Minister of Death: The Adolf Eichmann Story* (New York: The Viking Press, 1960), p. 157.

2. Randolph L. Braham, *The Politics of Genocide: The Holocaust in Hungary*, vol. II (New York: Columbia University Press, 1981), p. 945.

3. From The Trial of Adolf Eichmann, Session 61, *The Nizkor Project*, n.d., <http://www.vex.net/~nizkor/hweb/people/e/eichmannadolf/transcripts/Sessions/Session–061–04.html> (January 28, 2004).

Chapter 6. The Defeat of Nazi Germany

1. Jochen Von Lang and Claus Sibyll, eds., *Eichmann Interrogated: Transcripts from the Archives of the Israeli Police* (New York: Da Capo Press, 1999), p. 256.

2. Zvi Aharoni and Wilhelm Dietl, *Operation Eichmann: The Truth about the Pursuit, Capture, and Trial* (New York: J. Wiley, 1997), p. 45.

3. John Donovan, *Eichmann: Mastermind of the Holocaust* (New York: Kensington Publishing Group, 1978), pp. 199–201.

4. Quentin Reynolds, *Minister of Death: The Adolf Eichmann Story* (New York: The Viking Press, 1960), p. 185.

5. Aharoni and Dietl, p. 69.

6. Isser Harel, *The House on Garibaldi Street* (New York: Viking Press, 1975), pp. 2–3.

Chapter 7. The Search for Eichmann

1. Quentin Reynolds, *Minister of Death: The Adolf Eichmann Story* (New York: The Viking Press, 1960), pp. 203–204.

2. "Eichmann: From Capture to Trial," *The Trial of Adolf Eichmann*, n.d., <http://www.pbs.org/eichmann/study3.htm> (October 18, 2004).

Chapter 8. The Trial of Adolf Eichmann

1. Quentin Reynolds, *Minister of Death: The Adolf Eichmann Story* (New York: The Viking Press, 1960), p. 13.

2. Jochen Von Lang and Claus Sibyll, eds., *Eichmann Interrogated: Transcripts from the Archives of the Israeli Police* (New York: Da Capo Press, 1999), p. xxxi.

3. Ibid., p. 291.

4. Reynolds, p. 19.

5. Hannah Arendt, *Eichmann in Jerusalem: A Report on the Banality of Evil* (New York: Penguin Books, 1994), pp. 208–209.

6. Ibid., p. 223.

7. Ibid., p. 229.

8. From The Trial of Adolf Eichmann, Session 16, *The Nizkor Project*, n.d., <http://www.vex.net/~nizkor/hweb/ people/e/eichmann-adolf/transcripts/Sessions/Session-016- 01.html> (January 27, 2004).

9. From The Trial of Adolf Eichmann, Session 17, *The Nizkor Project*, n.d., <http://www.vex.net/~nizkor/hweb/ people/e/eichmann-adolf/transcripts/Sessions/Session- 017–01.html> (January 27, 2004).

10. PBS Online, "Eichmann's Final Plea," *The Trial of Adolf Eichmann*, n.d., <http://www.remember.org/eichmann/own words.htm> (April 29, 2005).

11. Arendt, p. 244.

Glossary

Aktion Reinhard—The nickname, after SD commander Reinhard Heydrich, for the plan of mass extermination of the Jews within occupied Poland.

Einsatzgruppen Special Action Squads—Small commando units within the RSHA that followed the regular German army into occupied eastern Europe to carry out mass execution of Jews, Communists, and native Poles and Russians.

General Government—A territory of central Poland, occupied by Nazi Germany after the invasion of September 1939, but not incorporated into Germany itself.

Gestapo (Geheime Staatspolizei)—Nazi Germany's national police force, responsible for the arrest, interrogation, and punishment of all those considered enemies of the state.

Madagascar Plan—A program, advanced by Eichmann and other high Nazi officials, of mass transportation of European Jews to the island of Madagascar, off the southern coast of Africa.

Reichssicherheitshauptamt (RSHA)—Head Office of Reich Security, the branch of Nazi government that commanded police and security forces, including the SD and the Gestapo.

Schützstaffel (SS)—An organization combining the elite military, security, and intelligence forces of Nazi Germany, open only to the most dedicated and loyal soldiers, spies, and policemen.

Section IV B 4—A branch of the RSHA and the Gestapo (Section IV). Section IV B 4 was headed by Adolf Eichmann and was responsible for planning and coordinating the capture and transportation of Jews throughout Europe.

Sicherheitsdienst (SD)—A branch of the SS originally founded as a top-secret intelligence-gathering organization, but later, under Reinhard Heydrich, responsible for putting into action the plan for the extermination of the Jews.

Vichy—The capital of unoccupied, southern France, where a wartime French government held authority in collaboration with Nazi Germany.

Wannsee Conference—A meeting of Nazi officials held in January 1942, in which Adolf Hitler and SD commander Reinhard Heydrich laid out plans for the extermination of the Jews in Europe.

Wehrmacht—Name for the regular German army during World War II.

Further Reading

Books on Adolf Eichmann

Dwork, Deborah, Harry Mulisch, and Robert Naborn. Criminal Case 40/61, *The Trial of Adolf Eichmann: An Eyewitness Account.* University of Pennsylvania Press, 2005.

Goni, Uki. *The Real Odessa: How Peron Brought the Nazi War Criminals to Argentina.* New York: Granta, 2002.

Gouri, Haim and Alan Mintz. *Facing the Glass Booth: Reporting the Eichmann Trial.* Wayne State University Press, 2005.

Levy, Alan. *Nazi Hunter: The Wiesenthal File.* New York: Carroll & Graf, 2002.

Sachs, Ruth. *Adolf Eichmann: Engineer of Death.* New York: Rosen Publishing Group, 2001.

Steinhouse, Carl L. *Wallenberg is Here! The True Story About How Raoul Wallenberg Faced Down the Nazi War Machine and the Infamous Eichmann and Saved Thousands of Budapest Jews.* Authorhouse, 2002.

Yablonka, Hanna and Ora Cummings. *The State of Israel v. Adolf Eichmann.* Shocken, 2004.

Books on Nazi Germany

Aarons, Mark and John Loftus. *Unholy Trinity: The Vatican, the Nazis, and Soviet Intelligence.* New York: St. Martin's Press, 1998.

Bessel, Richard (ed.) *Life in the Third Reich.* New York: Oxford University Press, 2001.

Evans, Richard. *The Coming of the Third Reich.* New York: The Penguin Group, 2004.

Gellately, Robert. *Backing Hitler: Consent and Coercion in Nazi Germany.* New York: Oxford University Press, 2002.

Goldensohn, Leon and Robert Gellately. *The Nuremberg Interviews.* New York: Random House, 2004.

Kaplan, Marion A. *Between Dignity and Despair: Jewish Life in Nazi Germany.* New York: Oxford University Press, 1999.

Mitchell, Allan. *Nazi Revolution: Hitler's Dictatorship and the German Nation.* Boston: Houghton Mifflin College Division, 1997.

Paxton, Robert O. *The Anatomy of Fascism.* New York: Knopf Publishing Group, 2004.

Sax, Benjamin C. and Dieter Kuntz. *Inside Hitler's Germany: A Documentary History of Life in the Third Reich.* Boston: Houghton Mifflin College Division, 1992.

Shirer, William L. *The Rise and Fall of the Third Reich: A History of Nazi Germany.* New York: Simon and Schuster, 1990.

Spielvogel, Jackson J. *Hitler and Nazi Germany: A History.* Upper Saddle River, NJ: Prentice Hall, 2000.

Books on the SS

Browder, George C. *Hitler's Enforcers: The Gestapo and the SS Security Service in the Nazi Revolution.* New York: Oxford University Press, 1996.

Hohne, Heinz and Richard Barry. *Order of the Death's Head: The Story of Hitler's SS.* New York: Penguin USA, 2001.

Jaskot, Paul B. *Architecture of Oppression: The SS, Forced Labor, and the Nazi Monumental Building Economy.* London: Routledge, 2000.

MacLean, French L. *The Camp Men: The SS Officers Who Ran the Nazi Concentration Camp System.* Atglen, PA: Schiffer Publishing, 1999.

MacLean, French L. *The Field Men: The SS Officers Who Led the Einsatzkommandos—the Nazi Mobile Killing Units.* Atglen, PA: Schiffer Publishing, 1999.

Padfield, Peter. *Himmler: Reichsführer-SS.* New York: Henry Holt, 1991.

Rhodes, Richard. *Masters of Death: The SS-Einsatzgruppen and the Invention of the Holocaust.* New York: Vintage Books, 2003.

Books on the Holocaust

Bauer, Yehuda and Nili Keren. *A History of the Holocaust.* New York: Franklin Watts, 2002.

Berenbaum, Michael. *The World Must Know: The History of the Holocaust as Told in United States Holocaust Memorial Museum.* Boston: Little, Brown, 1993.

Bitton-Jackson, Livia. *I Have Lived a Thousand Years: Growing Up in the Holocaust.* New York: Simon and Schuster, 1999.

Boas, Jacob. *We are Witnesses: Five Diaries of Teenagers Who Died in the Holocaust.* New York: Scholastic, 1996.

Browning, Christopher R. *Ordinary Men: Reserve Police Battalion 101 and the Final Solution in Poland.* New York: Perennial, 1993.

Dawidowicz, Lucy. *A History of the Holocaust* (Library of Jewish Studies). Springfield, NJ: Behrman House Publishing, 1976.

Dwork, Deborah. *Holocaust: A History.* New York: W. W. Norton, 2003.

Eichengreen, Lucille. *From Ashes to Life: My Memories of the Holocaust.* San Francisco: Mercury House, 1994.

Friedlander, Henry. *Origins of Nazi Genocide: From Euthanasia to the Final Solution.* Chapel Hill, NC: University of North Carolina Press, 1997.

Gilbert, Martin. T*he Holocaust: A History of the Jews of Europe During the Second World War.* New York: Owl Books, 1987.

Goldhagen, Daniel Jonah. *Hitler's Willing Executioners: Ordinary Germans and the Holocaust.* New York: Vintage Books, 1997.

Höss, Rudolph, with Stephen Paskuly and Andrew Pollinger. *Death Dealer: The Memoirs of the SS Kommandant at Auschwitz.* Cambridge, MA: Da Capo Press, 1996.

Koonz, Claudia. *The Nazi Conscience.* Cambridge, MA: Belknap Press, 2003.

Levi, Primo and Stuart Woolf. *Survival in Auschwitz.* New York: Simon and Schuster, 1996.

Nyiszli, Miklos. *Auschwitz: A Doctor's Eyewitness Account.* New York: Arcade Publishing, 1993.

Rees, Laurence. *Auschwitz: A New History.* Philadelphia, PA: Perseus Publishing, 2005.

Roth, John. *The Holocaust Chronicle.* Lincolnwood, IL: Publications International, 2000.

Wyman, David. *The Abandonment of the Jews.* New York: Pantheon Books, 1984.

Internet Addresses

Eichmann: The Mind of a War Criminal

<http://www.bbc.co.uk>

Click on "History" at the left. Click on "Wars and Conflict." Click on "Genocide Under the Nazis." Scroll down and click on "Eichmann: Mind of a War Criminal." under "Related Articles."

The Nizkor Project: Adolf Eichmann

<http://www.nizkor.org>

Under "People from A to Z," click on "Adolf Eichmann."

PBS: The Trial of Adolf Eichmann

<http://www.remember.org/eichmann>

Index